FOSTERED

A Collection of Fan Tributes to the Creators, Crew and Cast of The Fosters

Collected and published by Rae Ann Johnson
Edited by Taylor Gates and Alex J. Eiseman
Cover art by August Osterloh

The opinions expressed in this book are solely those of the
individuals to which they are attributed. Some of these accounts do
not necessarily reflect the author's opinions, nor do they
necessarily reflect the opinions of "The Fosters" cast or crew.

Fostered Copyright © 2018 Rae Ann Johnson.

ISBN-13: 978-0-692-09783-0

A Note from Rae Ann Johnson

We are aware of some spelling and grammatical errors in this book that were left to keep the integrity of each contributor's tribute.

All proceeds from the sale of this book will be donated to Los Angeles area foster agencies and / or foster-related charities.

Fostered

Adjective

1. Encourage or promote the development of (something, typically something regarded as good).
2. Develop (a feeling or idea) in oneself.
3. Bring up (a child that is not one's own by birth).
4. To bring up a child with parental care.
5. To encourage or help grow.
6. To provide the care that a parent usually gives to a child.
7. Taking a child into your family for a period of time without becoming its legal parent.
8. To bring up with care.

Dedication

To all the other fans of *The Fosters* that I've had the pleasure to meet and hope to meet — thanks for sharing this journey together. We will be forever connected via our love for this show and the people who brought it to us for five seasons.

@1BrittanyLove

My name is Brittany Love (@1BrittanyLove), and I am a super fan of The Fosters. I've been part of The Fosters fandom since 2014. My entry into this fandom is all thanks to two foster sisters I used to have. They've been with the show since the beginning, and I just happened to pop up on them one day while they were watching an episode. My eyes were immediately glued to the TV screen!

As soon as I saw the pilot of The Fosters, I knew that I was about to become madly obsessed with this show. I made this show a priority in my life. I even made sure my college schedule didn't interfere with my Fosters time. I made sure I was home every Monday/Tuesday to catch the new episode. No one was allowed to bother me while my show was on. If it's not related to the Fosters, I don't want to hear it between 8pm and 9pm, alright?

Anyway, I love this show because of the many reasons everyone loves it. First of all, there is no other show in the world like this one. There's no family on TV like this one. I was so amazed to see a blended family of biological, foster, and adopted kids raised by an interracial lesbian couple. This snatched my edges off! I was all the way here for this. This family has been through everything all families go through. My main reason for loving this show so much is because I grew up in the foster care system from the time I was eight years old, and I was so happy to finally see a TV show addressing what it's like to be in the system and all the issues with the system.

I don't think this show would have been as incredible as it was if not for the amazing casting! The cast is truly the reason why I'm still watching this show! I love everyone in the show, especially Sherri Saum who plays Lena Adams Foster and Cierra Ramirez who plays Mariana Adams Foster. I can give many reasons as to why their characters are my favorite, but I would rather talk about how amazing Sherri and Cierra are as people outside of the show. I had the pleasure of meeting them a few times, and they are seriously the sweetest celebrities you could meet. When you talk to them, it's like talking to family or your best friends. They love and care about their fans so much, and they're super fans of their own fans! I don't think I've ever seen celebrities interact with fans the way Sherri and Cierra do. If I ever become a celebrity in the future, I would like to be just like them. I just want to give a huge shoutout to them and let them know that I'm blessed that they know of my existence and that I will be supporting them forever.

I also really love the producers of the show, Bradley and Peter. They interact with fans on a daily basis, and they're so sweet in person. They're the reason for this show! I will be supporting and fangirling over this show even after its last season. This show has a really special place in my heart, and I don't think any other show in the future will take that place away from the Fosters. This will always be my favorite show and one of the best things that has entered my life.

Love,
— Brittany Love

@1gretchen

The Fosters has made me realize that it is ok to be who I am and ok to love someone of the same sex. I am now married to my soulmate: the love of my life. I love the saying that Stef says to her father Frank, "who I love shouldn't be an issue for you or anyone else." Stef and Lena are my favorite, but I love them all.

— Joyce All

@1jswnow

This show helped me open doors that I was afraid to open. Not only did Stef's life speak to me, but Lena's did too in some ways. The characters are strong and courageous. The topics that the show deals with are real. Things are not always finished with a happy ending, as is real life. The cast and crew are very welcoming and engage the fans on so many levels.

Through Twitter, The Fosters has made us a family all over the world. I just want to say thank you to everyone — cast, crew, and creators. Thank you for helping so many of us live our true selves.

With love,
— Jenn Williamson

@5separatehearts

One summer day in 2013, I was painfully bored. I couldn't find anything to do, so I decided to head on over to Netflix. I contemplated starting a new show, and something called The Fosters caught my eye. Out of curiosity, I clicked the play button and started watching.

Within minutes, I was hooked. I couldn't stop watching. I couldn't believe that I'd found something to relieve me of my boredom. Usually with new shows I tend to lose interest after a couple episodes, but not this time. Within a few days, I'd finished the entire set of 10 episodes that had been released so far. I soon made a Twitter account hoping to find tweets from the cast and writers, never imagining that I'd meet some of my best friends on that account and even interact with the cast. I never imagined that the executive producer and one of the main writers of the show, mastermind Bradley Bredeweg, would follow me on Twitter. I quickly felt highly emotionally connected to the show and to the cast and even started an Instagram account to make edits for the show.

By 2014, when the second half of the first season aired, I started watching the episodes live, tweeting along with the cast and writing team. I became part of a fandom — my first one — connecting and interacting with fellow fans of the show who shared my passion for it.

Today, I want to say thank you to The Fosters for five years of absolutely heartbreaking, heartwarming, captivating, and truly beautiful television. In the most important years of my life, I grew alongside Callie, Jude,

Brandon, Mariana, and Jesus. I learned so incredibly much from my second mothers, Stef and Lena. And I cried, laughed, yelled, and jumped from joy almost every week. It's been a rollercoaster of emotions, a wild ride. I truly, truly mean it when I say this show is one of the BEST on television. It's more than a show — it's been a part of my life. And I can't thank you all enough for it. It'll be in my heart always: my forever family. #ThankYouTheFosters

With much love,
— Aditi

@alxstl

I stumbled upon The Fosters way back when. Living in Australia, we very rarely have access to US and Canadian television shows; if we do, it's months or even years after a season has aired. But of course, we find ways around that — streaming etc. It was one summer break, and I was off university for 3 months. I spent most of my time binge watching television shows and working out. At that point in my life, I was still somewhat closeted. I had just had my heart broken for the very first time and was living life shut off from the outside world. I was searching for understanding. A support system.

Something or someone that understood the pain and confusion I was feeling.

I searched "television shows with lesbian characters," and up popped a list. The Fosters was right at the top, and upon reading the synopsis I was sold. I binge watched the first season in record time because for the very first time (since my teenage viewing of The L Word) I felt understood. I was watching as stories played out that represented a life I saw for myself.

I was in my early twenties, knowing in the deepest part of my soul that I was gay, yet I was still scared and anxious to tell my parents. I had, years prior, floated the idea that I was bisexual, but that hadn't gone over too well so retreat back into the closet I did.

Until Stef and Lena gave me the key to unlock it.

For the last two years, I've had the complete honor of reviewing The Fosters. I've been able to write and express how a show has changed my life and the lives of others. But before I started writing, The Fosters helped me do something even bigger. The Fosters gave me the courage and strength to speak my truth.

Teri Polo, navigating the internal struggle Stef faced with her own sexuality, spoke to me on levels I don't think anyone will ever understand. Sherri Saum, being Lena and illustrating the fierce and unparalleled love she has for Stef, helped me realize that loving hard and deep and fast isn't always a bad thing. Teri and Sherri, aside from their characters, have been warriors and cheerleaders and unknowing forces of motivation and inspiration through everything I've done over the last few years. The storytelling of these two actresses has become some of my most favorite work. They've given my life meaning and a voice to stories so long before left untold. And for that, I am deeply grateful.

Bradley Bredeweg, Joanna Johnson, Peter Paige, Wade Solomon and every other creative behind these stories: I tip my hat to you. Thank you for continuing to write relevant, important, and true to life stories. Thank you for giving this aspiring writer continued inspiration and drive. Thank you for defining what television storytelling should be.

To the entire Fosters family, I cannot say enough about how much this show has moved me, how much it's strengthened me, and just how full my life is now because I found the strength to speak my truth, to live my life the way I wanted, and to love hard and without question. You will always mean more to me than you know.

— Alex Steele

@angelicanordin

Hi! My name is Angelica. I'm 21 years old and live in Sweden. I started watching The Fosters when I was 18 years old. It was the first-ever show I could honestly connect with and relate to for so many reasons.

The Fosters helped me find myself and figure my sexuality out. It made me feel accepted, like I could finally fit in. The Fosters gave me the courage to come out to my dad (who is extremely supportive), and today I'm out to my whole family, friends and whoever I may meet. My sexuality is no longer a confusion or a secret.

Being a part of The Fosters fandom has been such an amazing experience. The cast has always been so lovely, caring, and genuine. I've met so many wonderful people in the fandom, some that I know will be lifelong friends. I also met my wife, Anna, through the show. We started off as an LDR couple (from Sweden to England) but broke the distance for good 2.5 years ago when I moved to England to live with Anna and her family. We lived there for a little over a year before we decided on moving to our own place in Sweden. We now live here with our two puppies and just got married last September.

The show hasn't just brought us two together but both our families as well. Even though our families are in two different countries, they still find themselves traveling between the two so that we can all be united on special occasions. That is one thing our parents spoke about on our wedding day: how amazing it is that two big families from different countries with different languages and cultures have been brought together into this one, beautiful and happy family.

I honestly wouldn't be where I am today if it wasn't for the show. Thank you for sharing such true and honest stories that so many of us have been able to relate to. Thank you for being the reason I was able to meet the love of my life. Thank you for absolutely everything.

— Angelica Nordin

@annasnordin

Hi, I'm Anna!

I would just like to say a massive thank you to the entire Fosters cast, crew, producers, and just everyone who contributed to the show and made it even possible.

The Fosters absolutely changed my life. I started watching it shortly after it came out, and I was hooked instantly. I had never been able to relate to a show more. The Fosters provided so much diversity, love, and acceptance. I had only come out as queer a couple of years before, but the show gave me so much more confidence in who I am. I met so many amazing friends in the fandom.

Late 2014 I even met another girl in the fandom, Angel, who I ended up falling in love with. She lived in Sweden, I lived in England, so we formed a long-distance relationship. Luckily, we were able to visit each other quite a bit in the beginning of 2015 and then Angel moved in with me and my family later on that summer.

Fast forward to now. We moved to Sweden and got married. We have our own place and two adorable little dogs. We're living our dream lives and it's all thanks to you guys. If The Fosters wasn't a thing, neither of us would have crossed paths. So, thank you once again, from the bottom of my heart, for literally changing my whole entire life. It's been such an amazing, fun, emotional, beautiful journey, and although The Fosters is coming to an end, it will always hold a special place in my heart. Thank you for everything.

Love,
— Anna Nordin

@artsyfosters

Hi! So, I've been watching The Fosters ever since the 2nd season came out, and it's literally my everything. The show is sooo amazing, and the cast is so unbelievably funny and nice. (I talked to Kalama before.) I'm so glad that The Fosters exists.

— Shar Yang

@ashleythecrow

The Fosters means so much to me. It helped me get through high school and really encompasses me growing up and transforming my views on certain topics my family never talked about. This show changed the way I see the world, and it may sound cheesy, but it really changed my life. I believe that this cast and crew really is full of genuine people who want to make this world a better place and really will go so far in whatever they pursue after. Thank you for changing my views on this world and making me a stronger person. If it wasn't for this show, I would not be the person I am today pursuing my dreams. You all are my heroes.

— Ashley Crowell

@bexbee41

Thank you, Fosters! You are the definition of true love, strength, acceptance, bravery, etc.

Never in my 41 years of existence has anything affected me the way you have. I don't think or believe the way I used to. Now I think and believe for the better.

Teri Polo and Sherri Saum are my biggest inspirations! I know for sure it is 100% possible to love and be inspired by people you have never met. I may never be able to be completely who I am, but I will be happy knowing it is always possible.

— Rebecca Bullard

@breisbest

I found The Fosters by it being recommended to me on Netflix (lol), and since then I've been hooked!

I think I connected in a strong way to this show because I love drama, romance, and suspense, and this show is the ONLY show I know that gives suspense like it's free candy. The suspension! Most of the show ends in a freaking suspenseful way, and I love it!

If I could write the ending, it'd be Callie and Brandon ending up together someway and something dramatic like one of The Fosters dying.

I connect most with Callie because she loves art but doesn't really know who she is and what she's meant to do and neither do I.

I'd like the crew to know that I fucking love them all! The show is fucking amazing! My favorite episode was probably the season finale when Stef was shot. It was so dramatic and suspenseful.

My favorite scene was by far Callie and Brandon being together finally at Lena and Stef's wedding because I'm a hardcore Callie and Brandon shipper lol.

— Bre Pelchat

@BrendaVilla

Thank you for giving us this amazing show and for being an example for so many people around the world. Thank you for being my anxiety relief when I am having a hard time and for making a show that includes everyone.

You guys mean so much to me. I heart you.

— Brenda Villa

@Brody1Amy

I love The Fosters! I love all of the characters. Bradley Bredeweg and Peter Paige couldn't have picked a better cast.

What I love the most is the strong family bond created by the uniqueness in which they all become one family. Whether it is biological, adopted, or fostered, whether you are the same sex, heterosexual, or a single parent, it all comes down to LOVE.

The one line that makes my heart proud is when Stef is talking to her dad in his kitchen telling him, "who I love should not matter to you or anyone else." It was the deciding moment for me when I knew I needed to come out as bi. No other show has ever or will ever be this profound to me.

— Amy Brody

@brokenttyme87

Today they wrap up filming the last episode of my favorite show: The Fosters. Thank you all so much for giving us a home, an insight into what the foster system is really like, and giving us all a story we all can relate to in more ways than one.

I started watching this show from the day it aired, and I've loved every episode and every season. The show keeps me attached because I connect with all the characters for different reasons. The only thing I can't connect with is being a foster kid. I didn't understand the foster system until the day the show aired, and what caught my attention was the ending scene with Hayden Byerly and Maia Mitchell. I cried my ass off and I said to myself, "I'm tuning in every week." Why? Because I love the actors so very much.

Everyone who is on The Fosters I have seen in other shows and movies before The Fosters, so that's another reason why because I love the actors so very much and will continue to support and watch the projects they are in.

To Maia Mitchell, Hayden Byerly, Cierra Ramirez, David Lambert, Noah Centineo, Jake T. Austin, Danny Nucci, Sherri Saum, Teri Polo, Bradley Bredeweg, Tom Williamson, Rosie O'Donnell, Daffany Clark, Tom Phelan, Peter Paige, Jules Kovisars, Joanna Johnson, JLo, Gavin Macintosh, Kalama Epstein, and everyone else involved, I want to thank you all because each and every one of you touched everyone at home watching. You all are the reason why we love watching The Fosters. We all are the reason for you guys reaching 100 episodes.

God bless you all, and I can't wait to see the ending. As I always say #MustHaveTissuesAtAllTimesWhile-WatchingTheFosters. It's true, and I love you all for it. I can't wait for the series finale and also can't wait for the series premiere of the spinoff. Just like Kari Kimmel says: it's not where you come from; it's where you belong. And to quote Lena, "DNA doesn't make a family — love does." I will live by that always.

While I'm thanking The Fosters cast and crew, I feel the after show should get some thanks, too, with their reviews and predictions and amazing guests they have on the show. Thank you, Jeff Masters, Jillian Leff, Stephanie Giorgi, Hannah Prichard, and AfterBuzz TV.

So, to end this, I want to say again that I love you all and am sad to see The Fosters go, but all good things must come to an end and all good things must have a spinoff. So, like I said, yeah, I'm sad about The Fosters leaving but I'm happy for the spinoff show. Thanks again, everyone, for giving us this amazing show. Love you guys.

From one of the amazing fans,
— Terrence "T-Tyme" Palmer II

@CaitlinKillarn5

This show is an inspiration to me and everyone in our country. You guys bring up topics that really need to be addressed and talked about. We need a show like this more than anything because it helps so many people and so many around the country. This is our show, and these are our stories. This show gives people a voice and helps so many people. We need them more than anything, and this show shouldn't be off the air because it's a huge part of our lives. This is not just a show — it's our lives being told by this amazing cast and crew. I am sending this message because our voices should be heard and because you have made a huge difference in my life and in everyone else's lives. We will do anything to keep our show and our family on the air. Please keep The Fosters on the air.

— Caitlin Killarney

@CarrieO21

I first found about The Fosters on Netflix a year after it aired on TV. I watched the first 3 episodes and thought, "this is a good show." It wasn't until a year after that I thought, "let me finish what I started."

I guess I was a bit dubious at first, but I was absolutely hooked once I tuned back in. I could not believe it had taken me so long to get back to watching this incredible show. I can't even describe the exhilaration I felt when watching it. I talk about it so much. I know my friends and family get tired of me speaking about The Fosters, but it's that beautiful to me.

I was instantly drawn to this show because of several things. Being that it was about foster kids and I have two close friends who were foster kids, I felt like I could relate to what my friends where dealing with when they were growing up. Another reason that kept me coming back was because of the PASSION you could see in each actor/actress that played these characters. They really gave it their all, and I could see in every episode how important this message was.

I loved, loved, loved the cast and crew. I feel this is the perfect family. The writing, the creativity, the diversity, the message, the LOVE... you really don't see real shows like this on television. Two moms that just love their children no matter what.

I have to give it to everyone who played a part in The Fosters. I mean, they really focused on love and real-life problems. Some days I would literally just cry because I was so touched. I am 27 years old and I can honestly say this by far is one of my top 3 shows. I learned so much from this show, and it holds a very special place in my heart. I am so thankful to be able to experience this show. It has changed many people's lives as well as some people's opinions.

This past summer I flew to California to visit the studio set of The Fosters in Burbank. I ended up going to an award show while I was there and ran into Cierra Ramirez. She was absolutely so sweet. I was able to chat with her for a bit and get a picture. It made my heart so full.

I would have to say I connected most to the character of Lena. We share a lot of things in common, and I was really able to figure out some things about myself just watching Sherri perform as Lena. I always said that would be the type of mom I was because our personalities are so similar. It was so great watching someone on television who you could actually relate to, and I found that in Lena. Sherri is so beautiful inside and out. She has blessed me more than she knows, and I can't thank her enough.

I really just want to thank every single person involved in The Fosters. Everyone deserves recognition. I am so glad they never gave up and took a risk. This was the best thing to happen to television. Bradley and Peter and Joanna...thank you for making this happen, and never stop believing. You changed so many lives and brought together a big happy family full of love.

My question is: can we please have a Foster fan party with the cast and crew? I would surely come. I just want us all together to celebrate this wonderful masterpiece. I love The Fosters so much. Thanks for all your hard work and dedication.

Seriously guys, I thank you for all the long hours and early mornings. You put your all into it and I loved every bit of supporting you all. I look forward to seeing you all.

Here's to spreading more love! I stand with THE FOSTERS!

— Carrington Briggs

@charlib1983

I found The Fosters while flipping through channels and saw Teri Polo. I love her, started watching the show online to catch up, and loved it instantly!

I immediately related to Callie and loved her relationship with Stef. I would have liked to have had someone like Stef in my corner. I am adopted, I was in foster care, and I am gay, but I haven't come out because my family is so religious. I would be shunned, and rejection is a huge fear for me. It is with most adopted or foster kids. We put a wall up and don't let people get too close for fear of rejection or being hurt.

I love every scene between Stef and Callie. I have a few favorites, but my very favorite scene is when Callie helped her friend get out of prostitution and Stef said she was proud of her for calling her and Callie flips out. That whole scene hits so close to my heart, and my favorite line from Stef is, "there is nothing you can do to make us not want you. Nothing."

I even relate to the wanting to meet their birth parents. I have met my birth mother, but my biological father is dead. His name was Charlie, and he died in 1983. That's where my twitter name came from. I look just like him, but I will never meet him. It's hard to never meet someone you are so much like.

I am 1 of 7. My birth mother has rejected me again, and she won't get another chance to do it. My story is long and really hard to believe, but it is all true. I have been lied to by my birth mother several times. She wants me to remain a secret which I am not anymore. I met another man whom she said was my father and she knew the difference when she saw me. Anyway, I won't get into my whole story. If anyone wants to know the whole winding trail of finding my birth family, they can reach out to me.

I just love the whole show, but my love of Teri Polo is what caught my eye, and I'm so glad it did. I love the show because it is so on point with everything. I relate to everything! I love the show! I don't want the show to end ever, but I know it will someday. I would just want everyone to be happy and healthy if the end comes. Thanks for doing this tribute. It is well deserved

— Rosina Key

@chloebwallace

Hi. My name is Chloe, and I am 15 years old from New Zealand. I first started watching The Fosters in 2016 after I had been to America and went through the set house, never hearing of the show and not even knowing what it was about. Then I came home to find it on the

TV one afternoon. The Fosters was only up to season 3 then.

The thing that attracted me to The Fosters was the fact that it was led by two mums. It was so amazing to see two mums being portrayed on TV, and the show was so realistic. I think I connected to this TV show so strongly as my two aunties are gay and they are like mothers to me. I connected with Stef the most, as she reminds me of an older version of myself. She tries to get through a lot on her own, she feels like she doesn't need anyone, and she is a strong woman.

I also connected with Jesus as he is always the one getting called dumb and doesn't understand a lot at school even when he tries really hard, which I can relate to.

Teri Polo's character Stef influenced my life in a positive way and made me feel like it was okay to be myself, to cut my hair if I wanted too, and to open up to people. My favorite quotes from The Fosters are "DNA doesn't make a family — love does" by Lena. "We probably judge ourselves way harsher than anyone judges us," by Ana. And my all-time favorite by Stef, "who I love shouldn't be an issue for you or anyone else."

I love all of Teri and Sherri's tweets to each other. They are all so loving and adorable. I would just like to say that this show has opened up my eyes to so many things. It has changed me and made me a better person. I've never loved a show or anything so much in my whole life. It means everything to me.

I love how the show has covered so many things, such as LGBT issues, bullying, Alzheimer's, school shootings, relationships, love, family, and so much more. My favorite storyline was Stef being with Mike and leaving him for Lena, finally coming out and telling everyone she was gay, as I have had a family member do this.

I sometimes feel like I have to hide who I am, by being someone I'm not just for others around me. My favorite episodes in The Fosters is the first wedding episode. I loved this episode as it's full of so much love and happiness. Also, it was the day that gay marriage became legal in the U.S. I also loved Padre, as I may not know what it's like to lose a dad, but I do know what it's like to lose someone, and in that episode, I felt like I connected with Stef as she was trying to be really strong and acted like she was fine. I loved the scene in the Padre episode with Stef and Callie. The words that came out of Stef's mouth were so beautiful.

Teri Polo is my absolute favorite actress, and she means the world to me. She puts a smile on my face even when I'm down. Seeing her happy makes me happy and I don't know what I'd do without her. She keeps me going and makes me want to be a better person. When she got her hair cut short, I had never been so proud of her. She is a role model for so many people including me.

Bradley Bredeweg is also one of my inspirations. His work on The Fosters is incredible and outstanding. He is such an amazing guy, and I look up to him as a 15-year-old. Bradley is the most genuine, kind and compassionate man. Him and Teri never fail to stand up and speak up for what they believe in, which I admire. I love those two more than anything, from the bottom of my heart.

Love,
— Chloe Wallace

@closetodreaming

I was in middle school when The Fosters came out. I remember being with a friend and seeing a commercial and being like, "WE HAVE TO WATCH THAT!" Between my friend and I, we either knew at least one (but often more than one) person who was adopted, in or had been in juvie, was a foster child, had been in tough situations, was gay, and so many other things connected to the show, so I think we could really connect to what happened in it.

The best thing about this show is that it really shows life and how it can be tough, which a lot of shows don't really go into detail about or sugar coat. Also, it explores things like juvie, LGBT centers, foster care, adoptions, struggle, and shows both sides to every topic really well.

I connected to Callie the most because soon after the show started I ran away from home and went into the system. I struggled with a lot of things she goes through, and I could relate to the way she deals with things or relate to how she reacts when things aren't great. She gives me hope that I can overcome my own situations. My favorite episodes are when Callie does and shows her Senior Project. My favorite scene is Season 3, Episode 16 when Rita Hendricks and Callie have that heartfelt conversation about Rita's daughter.

Stef and Lena really influenced my life because they are who I want to strive to be when I am older. I have become more honest with my sexuality, and I want to have a family and be good parents like they are. I have always wanted to have foster kids when I am older and adopt and have my own kids. They also show that they aren't always perfect, and that means a lot to me.

I am new to Twitter, but I joined because I saw that Maia Mitchell posted "Renew the Fosters" on Facebook. I want all the cast members to know they all play the parts beautifully and really make a difference. To everyone who wrote the scripts: thank you for not being afraid to open people's eyes to what really happens and for making everything really relatable to the group of people that often get overlooked or viewed with a negative association in other shows/movies/plays.

I want to know: Maia, is it hard for you to play Callie? How has playing Callie changed your life or point of view?

— Alyssa St. Pierre

@costumesgal

Five years ago, I saw Stef Foster and Lena Adams on mainstream TV and realized the world was really changing. They are written and portrayed as three-dimensional women whose lesbian identities do not define them but are just naturally a part of who they are as women, mothers, professionals in their fields, and partners in their relationship. It validated the experience of myself and so many other middle-aged women who grew up in a time when we were not free to acknowledge all parts of ourselves and who felt the world would define us and defeat us because of our sexual identity.

As a bisexual woman in a healthy hetero marriage, I identified with Stef and Lena on so many levels. Their relationship mirrors my own and therefore crosses sexual identity lines. I can also identify with them as individuals, in that many of their experiences as moms, as parents of teens also mirror my own.

The message that sexual identity is not your only defining characteristic comes through loud and clear. I also really appreciate the message that in life it's really all about the love. That comes through loud and clear as well. I'm not sure there will ever be another couple that measures up to Stef and Lena on TV, but I'd love to see showrunners try.

— Terri Winters

@damnhyland / @MaiaMitchellFR

I discovered The Fosters thanks to social media. The whole cast attracted me to the show, and then when I knew about the storyline, I just HAD to watch.

This show taught me so many important things at a young age, and I could never thank them enough for this. The fact that it brings up so many educational topics is the best thing about the show. When the show ends, I want them all to be happy and stay strong af as a family.

The actor I connect with most is probably Cierra Ramirez. Even though I love them all, Cierra has had my heart since the beginning. She's so nice, funny, iconic and loving. She really cares about us. She was there when I needed it the most. I want her to know that I love her more than anything and she has a big place in my life.

The whole cast is amazing on Twitter. They use their platform to talk about amazing issues, but they are also funny on it.

My favorite storyline was when Mariana joined the dance team and wanted to fit in by dying her hair blonde. In the end, she taught the girls much more and she really started to be more confident. She inspired me to be that confident.

My favorite episode is Mother Nature because we could feel how much they considered themselves a family off camera. It was beautiful to watch — they were all so happy. My favorite scenes are when they're just being a family. Those are so important.

— Lea Lempereur

@DanyGamboa4

I found The Fosters on Netflix one night, and I thought, "why not?" The first episode was awesome, and I loved it.

The thing that attracted me the most is that everyone in the show had real problems. They used and showed this to cause the audience to have feelings. Callie's story is connected with me because she is always trying to solve social problems. I connected with Cierra Ramirez (Mariana) because I know how it feels to be an adopted girl with a drug addict mom. My favorite episode is season 3 episode 19.

The Fosters is a real show with real life problems. It has a lot of love and drama, and the actors can express the feelings and transmit it really well. This series is a ten!

From Colima Mexico, I want to send all my support and love to all the cast.

— Dany Gamboa

@DEldoriz

The reason for me watching The Fosters is that it gives me immense happiness just to see all the cast, the realistic stories, and the drama on my screen. I have watched every single episode more than 20-30 times. Even during hiatus, I watch 2 to 3 episodes of The Fosters every single night after I come back from work. It relaxes me a lot. I love my moms Stef and Lena soooo much. :)

— Dinns Fernandez

@dolanschampions

I was on Netflix, and I needed something new to watch. I had heard of the show prior to that day, and I had never heard anything bad about it. I decided to start watching it, and I really enjoyed it.

I think all of the rawness and drama attracted me to the show as well as how they included very important topics that are never talked about. I can see the emotion through the characters' eyes and it makes me feel as if this family is real. The best thing is how much emotion is shown in every episode.

I think I can connect with each character on a different level, but if I had to choose one, I would say Callie. She's been through a lot and tries to make everyone happy. She puts herself through tough situations in order to save others. She doesn't realize how much of an impact she makes on other people, and she enjoys art a lot. She's just like me. She also taught me that I need to stand up for myself. I've been bullied all of my life and I've never learned how to stand up for myself. Once I started watching this show, I realized that I can't let others put me down.

My favorite tweet from one of the actors is, "Smile, that shit is more contagious than the flu" by Noah Centineo.

I want Cierra to know that she makes me happy. I named my dog after her character on The Fosters (you liked and RT'ed that tweet), and she is now almost a year old and is happy. I'd love to meet you one day, and it's my dream to act in a TV show or movie with you!

The episode that got me the most was season 4, episode 1. Every time I watch it, I cry right when Mariana is found and is being walked out of the school and Jesus hugs her.

— Destiny Lanning

@Dreamer1289

Wow. What can I say about The Fosters? It's an amazing show. I was about 21 years old when I heard about this show. I had read about it, and it captivated me from the start. I can relate to this show because I was adopted. I went into foster care at 10 months old. I had been neglected and God only knows what else happened to me.

I got to go back to my birth mother for a year-and-a-half but then she lost me again. I was finally adopted around the age of 5 by a wonderful couple who had six kids at the time. Two of the kids were adopted. The others were biological.

I saw my birth mother twice a year because it was an open adoption. Being adopted was the best thing that ever happened to me. I still don't understand why I was neglected and left alone from time to time. Even now, at 27 years old, I still don't know what I did wrong. I ask myself questions like, "Was I a bad baby? Did I cry too much? Was I not good enough?" I just don't get it. Only people who have been adopted or in foster care would understand where I am coming from.

Although I have incredible parents, I still often wonder what was going on in my birth mother's head when she had me. The Fosters helped me accept the fact that I can't change anything. Everything that happened in my life obviously happened for a reason.

This show has taught me that I'm not the only one who has gone through hard times. I still have moments where I wish I could go back in time. All I can do now is just keep living my life the best that I can. I don't think I will ever get over the fact that my own birth mother neglected me and didn't care about me. If she had wanted me, she would have fought hard to get me back.

Watching The Fosters helped me make more friends, some who I now call family. It's so amazing how this TV show brought so many strangers together and formed a family. I hope The Fosters stays around forever. I know where I come from, but The Fosters family is where I belong.

— Erica Killian

@duncszim

To all the cast and crew, past and present: thank you so much for an amazing and inspiring show, in particular for the amazing development of characters in so many respects. May the show continue forever. I am not one for singling out generally, but my favorite character is Jude (Hayden Byerly, you legend!) Lots of love.

— Duncan Cumming

@ebro75

The day I started following people in The Fosters fandom changed my life. I've met wonderful people because of the show. Our love for Teri Polo narrowed our group down to a handful, and the Polosgroupies were born. We would tweet each other till the wee hours in the morning talking about the show and what direction we thought the characters were going, it was like therapy.

I finally got to meet some Polosgroupies in person and made friends for life. It's amazing how our love from one show brought hundreds of us from across the globe together. It was a fantastic feeling to be able to hug someone you never thought you would ever meet!

I'll never forget my New York vacation for a few reasons. Firstly, I got to go to NYC thanks to Tammy. I got to meet Erin, Darby, Cali, Terri, and Deb for the first time. I was in a Taxi on New Year's Eve on my way to a bar with Tammy and Deb when Teri followed us on Twitter. That was a fantastic feeling!

I've never seen a cast talk to their fans like the cast of the Fosters. If not for The Fosters, I would have never met the amazing and wonderful people in my life. The people I'm proud to call my friends, we may not talk every day, we may not have met in person yet, but they are still my friends.

Teri, Sherri, Bradley, and Peter (to name a few): thank you from the bottom of my heart. Without y'all and The Fosters, my life would be so different. I would have never gotten to meet Tammy, Lisa, Stephanie, Houston, Erin, Cali, Terri, Deb and Darby in person.

The rest of my Polosgroupies and my Booville peeps I've never met in person but maybe one day. I've connected with people I would have never met thanks to The Fosters. I will forever be grateful and a fan for life! Fosters Fandom is the bomb dot com! Love y'all.

— Erica Breaux

@Elphaba_Anne

To be completely honest, I stumbled upon The Fosters by accident during a vacation the summer before my senior year of high school. Being a night owl, I was up hours after my family had gone to sleep. Bored and wide awake, I scrolled through iTunes and saw a free pilot of this little ABC Family show that had just premiered. It sounds cheesy and dramatic, but my life really did change at 1 a.m. in that Floridian condo.

I could ramble for hours about all the ways this show has impacted me, but I'll try my best to keep it short and sweet. These characters have been with me during so many huge moments in my life. When I went off to college, studied abroad, and moved to a city I had never been for a summer, there was always something so comforting and empowering about having Stef's pep talks, Lena's soothing words, Callie's courage, and Mariana's confidence just a click away. Lena's quote in a season one episode, "you can't live your life in fear of what might happen," immediately became — and will likely forever remain — my life motto.

Seeing a happy, healthy lesbian couple onscreen played a huge part in finally allowing myself to explore and eventually embrace my sexuality. But the support and kindness I received from this show's fans was even more important. It truly made me start to think about my sexuality in a different way—being gay isn't something I should have to apologize for or feel awkward about; it's a part of me and should be celebrated. The relationships I've built online and off due to our shared love for The Fosters is something so special and unique.

I will be forever grateful for the encouragement the entire cast and crew has shown me. You have no idea how much your generosity, advice, and love mean. I will never, ever be able to thank every single one of you enough for all the opportunities you've given me throughout these years. Thanks to you, so many of my dreams have become a reality, and you have inspired me to work to make even more of my wildest goals possible.

Love always,
— Taylor Gates

@EngenEn

I found The Fosters by searching Netflix in the spring of 2016. (So, I was a little late.) I was attracted to the show because of the credibility of the characters. I became strongly attached to the show because it showed that gay people also can raise a family. The best thing about this show is that the world gets to see that gay people are equal to everyone else. I love all of the characters. I think every one of the actors have influenced my life by playing their characters really well.

I love tweets from Sherri, Teri, and Maia when they promote things like women's right, dogs that need help, and children in Africa. They are important, and their tweets teach many people.

I would like the actors and crew members to know that the story they are telling is important and significant for the whole world. I have a hard time picking a favorite storyline, a favorite scene, or a favorite episode. I think all of it is very good.

— Tone Engen

@fostersfanpaige

I love Stef/Teri Polo all the way because she is an AMAZING TALENTED ACTRESS! I love the cast and crew because they are amazing!

I am a big fan!

— Kristine Thomas

@fostersonellend

One day at the beginning of January 2017, I got on Netflix. For the first time ever, The Fosters was just sitting there under Top Picks, and I said, "What the hell? I need a new show to watch." So, I clicked it.

Now, I had heard the name before, but I never knew what the show was about or who was in it. By the second episode, I was hooked. Episode by episode I was in awe and couldn't believe I didn't know that a show like this existed. And here I am a few months later, not only trying to get the cast on The Ellen Show (haha), but also a part of this amazing family called The Fosters Fam.

The Fosters is a show that has truly given me a whole new outlook on life. It has taught me so many different lessons, but overall that it's okay. It's okay to be who you are, it's okay to be confused, it's okay to love this or that person, it's okay to stand up for what you believe in, it's okay to be you. At the end of the day, LOVE IS LOVE.

I'm forever grateful for the cast, producers, and crew for all of the hard work and love they have given us all these years. Thank you so much. And to the Fosters Fam, thank you for the constant love and support while trying to make #fostersonellen happen. You guys motivate me every day to keep going and not give up. I love you guys. We'll make it happen one of these days!

I gotta wrap this up because I could go on forever. That one click changed everything and I'm now right where I belong and couldn't be happier. The Fosters will forever hold a special place in my heart.

— Linda Clark

@frnakcaslte

I started watching The Fosters when I was around fourteen, and without the influence of it, I would not be who I am today. It has shaped me as a person over the last three years, and I could not be more grateful for every single episode. The amount of laughs, tugs at my heart, and ugly sobs I have given to this show is beyond high, but I wouldn't have it any other way.

This show has educated me on things that have affected me in life and taught me to be strong in moments I never thought I could be. It is a wonderfully groundbreaking and authentic show that needs to be on our TV screens, presenting problems and issues that other media outlets are too scared to. I am so proud to call myself a fan.

My favourite episode was 2x18, mainly because the Jonnor storyline was my favourite. I took that storyline to heart and took pride in the amount of publicity it gained, and I was so thankful for the representation that it gave. Similarly, the LGBT+ prom episode was another favourite. It was so different and inspiring that it had me bursting with pride and happiness. This show never falls short on representation, and I'm so thankful that it reaches minorities and gives them hope.

Familial bonds are one of my favourite things to see on TV, which I think is why I connected with this show so strongly. Stef and Lena's relationship, to name one, is one of the healthiest domestic f/f relationships I have ever seen on TV, and for all of the issues surrounding lesbian representation in the media, this show never fails to go above and beyond.

Thank you. Thank you for such a wonderful show that I know I will watch until it goes off air, rewatch until the end of eternity, pass onto my kids when I am older. As an aspiring writer, I look up to Brad and Peter and all the other writers on this show for creating such strong-willed and passion-filled content. I hope to raise awareness and provide representation just like they do.

Thank you from the bottom of my heart, I hope that this show gains all the appreciation and success that it deserves.

— Olivia Chalmers

@FullerKeirstan

Dear The Fosters cast,

Y'all are one of my favorite shows to ever go on TV. Y'all's show has given me something to look forward to. I've watched y'all's show about seven times on Netflix.

P.S. My fav couple has to be Brallie💗 💗 Love y'all to the moon and back!!!

— Keirstan Fuller

@happylittlefl

I found The Fosters when I was just a preteen. I remember I thought it was so good and just had to keep watching. I think I am connected because it deals with situations with such compassion, and it never ceases to amaze me.

I connected the most with Callie because I have been through a lot of experiences that she has been through. She really influenced me to be stronger. My favorite video that Maia posted was her drinking coffee and basically loving on David. My favorite storyline was Callie getting Jude out of that foster home because she showed so much power and love in that scene.

— Faith Adams

@hiimbec

Dear Fosters Cast (especially Teri, Sherri, and Bradley),

I want you all to hear my story. I'm a pastor's daughter. My dad has been a Baptist preacher my whole life. My mom had been a youth minister at the same church. We live in Virginia, and basically, I was raised in a homophobic, conservative family.

I noticed something was off from the start. My first celebrity crush was Sharon Osborne. I would always find girls pretty, and I would always be friends with the boys only because I was shy around the girls.

When my parents noticed something was off about me, they didn't take it well. They knew what it was. They've never said it out loud, but I know that they knew.

I lived in fear, in disappointment, hating myself. Then, your show.

I moved across the state last year, and I had to leave my friends behind and make friends in a town full of rich, privileged, white people who had confederate flags on their trucks, hated gay people, and worshipped Donald Trump.

I started your show around that time. I was in a severe depression, because I knew I wouldn't be accepted where I was. Not by my family, and not by my new friends.

Your show gave me family. I became emotionally invested in each individual character. Like Stef and how her father was homophobic. Like Jude and how he found a church that loved and accepted him. Like Noah, who was gay and a pastor's son. I found myself becoming happy and having a family to be with and watch after school.

I love to research actors of characters and shows I love, but a lot of times I'll watch interviews, and the actors are just that: actors. When I watched Teri and Sherri, they weren't just actors. They genuinely loved each other.

Seeing that love on screen, and knowing it was truly genuine, made my life light up completely.

I used to be transphobic, because I never understood it. Now, my views are completely different because I saw Callie dating Aaron!

Whenever my parents would say something to tear me down or whenever I couldn't make friends at my new school, I would go home and watch Teri and Sherri. Every single Tuesday, I would Tweet Bradley, and every time he responded I was convinced we were best friends. I would literally lay in bed at night thinking that if I ever had a "Make A Wish," I'd want to meet Teri, Sherri, and Bradley. I guess that's a strange, morbid, and quite possibly offensive thing to say, but I'm being honest.

For Teri and Sherri's love for each other, for Sherri's tweets every Tuesday (even though she has never noticed me), for Teri's laugh, for how much Bradley would tweet me, for the one-time Peter Paige said happy birthday to me, for every storyline that I could relate to, and for being the family I never had: thank you.

I'm not out yet. My parents haven't come around to the fact that I'm gay. Although I haven't told them, I know they know.

I wish Teri and Sherri had a spin off. Random and off topic, I know. I just thought I should squeeze it in there.

Thank you. Thank you for being my everything. You literally saved my life. I was suicidal, depressed, and angry. Then I realized that I did have a family out there.

The Adams Foster family and the Fosters cast. I love you all,
— Becca Mullins

@HudsonMaloria

I love this show. There are so many great things to learn from it. Love is love, all we have to do is accept it.

— Maloria Hudson

@iamnotyourlawyr

The older we get, the more we begin to recognize our own patterns. For me, every few years I find myself bored – with work, with hobbies, with my day-to-day existence. It's at these times that I begin to look around for the next thing that's going to capture my attention and provide a mental escape. Sometimes it's a new hobby. Sometimes it's a place I find myself returning to again and again.

In the summer of 2013, bored and frustrated, I was absently flipping channels when I came upon a show I'd never seen or even heard of before. I wish I could remember exactly which episode was playing that caught my eye and made me stop and watch. It was an episode of season 1A, and I soon found myself watching an all-day marathon of 1A that culminated in the unforgettable wedding of Stef and Lena.

Now, I'm one of those, "older" fans. I had never before (or, really, since) watched an ABC Family/Freeform show. The teenage stuff was fine – even fresh. But it was the undeniable chemistry between the moms that captivated me.

I realized that I was receiving a validation I wasn't aware I needed. Though I'd been "out" for nearly a decade by then and had been with my now-wife for five years, there were still plenty of circumstances in which I hesitated to let people know my whole truth. But I always felt somehow dishonest when I "neglected" to mention my girlfriend in certain business and social situations.

Seeing a version of my life represented on television made me realize how much that internal conflict impacted me. I didn't realize until I saw Stef and Lena together that they represented a vision of my own dream life that had never before appeared on American television. Stef and Lena reminded me that I'm not "throwing my sexuality in someone's face" when I speak of my family. I'm just living my own life, like everybody else. I'm as average and ordinary, and as special and unique, as every other person in this world. It's precisely the ordinariness of the Adams Foster family that makes them so relatable.

Thank you to Bradley Bredeweg, Peter Paige, Joanna Johnson, Teri Polo, and Sherri Saum, and all the people who play a part in bringing this extraordinarily ordinary family to us and reminding us all that our most important role in life is, as Sherri is fond of saying, to just "Be you, Baby."

— Meg Tebo

@irp1313

I started watching The Fosters because my Netflix account said I had a 94% compatibility with it. I was in between shows because I had finished watching Glee for the 7th time. I knew Maia from Teen Beach Movie and Jake T. Austin from Wizards of Waverly Place (I know it's really dorky), so I was like, "ok, I'll watch it."

After the first couple of episodes, I fell in love. I loved the diversity of the show and acknowledging the foster care system. I personally am not part of the LGBTQIA community, but I am someone who does not tolerate any hate towards anyone because they aren't "normal." I believe there is no normal — everyone is unique — and I feel that The Fosters exemplifies that in such a great way.

I love Jesus as a character, and I could not have been happier that they recast him because The Fosters without Jesus would have been so sad. Noah, you are an amazing actor, whether that be your ability to show emotion or your amazing portrayal of someone with a TBI.

Ok, so I personally am still a Jonnor shipper through and through. I loved Connor and Jude together, but now

Joah is just goals. Hayden, I love Jude. Plain and simple. You do such a great job of bringing him to life, and I'm thankful to you for that. Kalama, what can I say?! When Jude originally started to date Noah I was like, "ugggghhhhh whyyyyyyy?" And then I got to meet Noah, who you brought to life. I was like, "the pastor's son is gay. That doesn't fit." You are so awesome, and you and Hayden together are hilarious!

Maia and Cierra, you two are so great together. The fact that you are best friends in real life and play sisters on the show is amazing. My best friends are basically my family, so seeing you both in real life and onscreen warms my heart. Mariana and Callie are both such spitfires. I give Mariana and Cierra so much credit for all the work they have to do for roller derby. Maia, your American accent for Callie is so good. Honestly, if I didn't know that you were Australian then I would think your American accent was just your regular voice.

David, holy cow! Your piano skills are insane. I play piano but just for fun — not anything serious. And then there's Brandon/you, who is a genius and is amazing. Your voice is great...now you have to learn to dance and you could be a triple threat!

Danny, what can I say?! I love Mike. He's such a lovable guy, and you seem the same way! You are an amazing director as well.

THE MAMAS!!!!!! Sherri and Teri, I don't even know what to say. You ladies are so empowering, and the show wouldn't be the show without you two. You both show the ups and downs of relationships with Lena and Stef. I remember reading the article about how you two went as each other's dates to the GLAAD Awards and how amazing that was. You two are such courageous women, and I thank you for that.

The way this show keeps up with current events keeps me coming back every time. All in all, thank you to everyone who has contributed to this amazing show. You all are awesome and have made this show what it is.

— Isabella Pfannenbecker

@Jdub_0752

Where do I begin? To start at the beginning of my journey with The Fosters is to go back to a time when I was completely lost in my life. And going back to the beginning where my love for them began brings back a flood of memories, some that make me smile and others that make me weep. Yet to clearly understand my personal journey, one must acknowledge the fact that a beginning had to start somewhere.

I was living in West Virginia at the time, about 5 hours from where I grew up, and it was a very depressing time in my life. I had recently lost my job working for The Board of Childcare, working with troubled teens for over 27 months, and to say I was burnt out was an understatement. Seeing the previews of The Fosters caught my attention only because I was curious if they would depict the foster system correctly and what these kids do go through. I was not only pleased to see they had gotten it right on every level, but also that they had intertwined a loving family setting that tugged at one's heart strings.

I had a Twitter account which I never used, and one evening while watching on ABC Family, on the bottom of the screen was a caption inviting fans to live tweet with the cast. I was completely lost to say the least, yet I watched the tweets that flooded my timeline left and right. I soon saw people from all over the world had one thing in common: The Fosters Family. And I was excited to begin to interact with them.

It was all very overwhelming to me at first as I'd sit at my laptop and watch conversations take place between all of these people, and the fact that I somehow was tagged in a few conversations, made me want to hyperventilate because I couldn't keep up. But I met some really cool people who are still, to this day, good friends of mine. And through this network of people, I have come to really understand that "blood doesn't always make a family, but love does."

When my father died suddenly in May of 2015, a group of my friends all took pictures of their hands and made a collage, tagging me in the post saying they were holding my hand, and I could literally feel the love and support they exuded to me from around the country.

Even to this day, I look to The Fosters as a pivotal point where I began to find the help I needed to find myself and essentially who I am. I have come to accept myself and am still learning to love myself in ways I never saw possible. I have learned that love really is that: LOVE, and it doesn't always necessarily fit into a box. There isn't always rhyme or reason to it. It just is. And I look towards Teri Polo for a lot of the wisdom I took away to use in my everyday life.

I felt so drawn to Teri because of her humanity and the love she shared with her fans. I hated it when everyone began to try to fight for her attention because I wouldn't want to be in her shoes trying to get to everyone and be fair about it while doing so. I saw almost immediately her love and compassion… how very kind she was, and her heart filled with desire to help those who were struggling. And back then, I was one of the ones who was spiraling out of control and fast. When I hit rock bottom, I realized that no one really could help me but myself. I had to come to the realization that in order to get back up, I had to yank myself up by the bootstraps and make myself get the help I so desperately needed.

Teri, I want you to know and understand just how great of an impact you had on my life. I will forever be grateful for being around when you were on Twitter and would impart your wisdom to us on a weekly basis. I saw how sensitive you are, and I saw pieces of myself in you. I completely get your heart, and how hard you love people. For a while, I did set you up on a pedestal, but as I began to grow as a person, I realized that setting someone on a pedestal is setting them up to fall at some point. It's better to look at someone you admire as your equal…as a normal human like the rest of us who laughs and cries and has good and bad days. Thank you, Teri, for all you have given through your character, Stef Adams Foster, and through your normal self, Teri Polo.

I want to close by thanking Sherri Saum as well. The way you depicted Lena Adams Foster was exceptional. I loved Lena's passion for youth and how she knew how to get on their level. I also loved watching the amazing chemistry that Sherri and Teri brought not only on the screen but also off in real life. Their friendship will forever be my favorite, selfless depiction of what I view friendship to be.

This will most likely go down in history as my all-time favorite TV show and into my personal memoirs as having had a hand in changing my life. "It's not where you come from, it's where you belong. Nothing I would change. I wouldn't have it any other way..."

— Elizabeth A. Hamm

@Jess072417

Without the cast and crew of The Fosters, I wouldn't be where I am today. I never would've met Teri Polo or been introduced to Laura Marie Live. I also wouldn't have found the strength to get help for my mental health issues and suicidal thoughts. I never would've been able to come clean about lies I had told or to receive help I desperately needed. I also wouldn't believe I am worth being accepted or loved.

I feel like I have found a family with The Fosters, one I've always dreamed of, one where I am truly loved and accepted for who I am. I've learned that I do not have to hide or lie about who I am in order to be accepted and loved for who I truly am.

This show is helping thousands of people every day regardless of race, religion, age, sexuality, wealth, or gender, and I am thankful to all of the cast and crew who bring this show to life each season and who continue to help this family we have created.

— Jessica Malott

@joshroot_

The Fosters means a lot to me. Although I didn't watch it when it first started, I binged the first season on Netflix a night in 2014 and started watching live when season 2 aired its summer premiere. It's taught me several life lessons and tackled topics and issues that I didn't know about before.

It's taught me that it's okay to be who you are, and you shouldn't be ashamed of yourself for it — people will love you regardless. DNA doesn't make a family: love does. I won't only miss the show, but I'll miss the live tweeting every week, behind-the-scenes photos, sneak peeks, and the cast.

The Fosters will always be a part of my life, and because of it, I have met some amazing people and the fandom has created a big family within itself. The Fosters will live on forever, and I think more and more people will continue getting into it and understand what it's about. It's one of those shows that shouldn't go unnoticed, especially in today's society. "It's not where you come from — it's where you belong."

— Josh Root

@jumpthanfxll

Hi, my name is Sarah, and I'm a huge fan of *The Fosters*! I started watching the show when it first aired, and I was captivated by the uniqueness of the show. I was soon enchanted by the ideas that the show presented as well as the wide range of powerful topics the story lines covered.

I believe I first connected with the show because I now identify as pansexual, and throughout the years that I watched the show I was struggling to figure out my sexuality. Watching the show and seeing how Stef and Lena dealt with their sexualities and lived a normal life made me feel more confident in who I am.

Personally, I had connected with Ashley Argota (Lou) who was on the show and thankfully had the opportunity to meet her twice. I'm thankful she was a guest star on the show because I loved her character and the challenge she posed to the characters in the show (such as Brandon), and I also appreciate how caring and generous she is in real life.

Due to the show, I was able to make many friends as I was actively involved with the fandom on Twitter. I happened to also meet my best friend through the fandom, and I will be forever grateful to *The Fosters* for bringing us together.

Ultimately, I would like to thank each and every one of the cast and crew for adding something special to the show and making it one of the most revolutionary television shows of my generation. Myself and many others are extremely thankful for everything *The Fosters* brought to us, and how it helped shape us as people. *The Fosters* will always remain in my heart. I wish the best to everyone continuing their careers after the show. It will be missed.

Thank you for taking the time to read this,
— Sarah Sloan

@justindefend

When I first watched The Fosters, I thought it was going to be just one more TV show on my list. But it was more than that. I have feelings for this show. It is like my home, and home is a place you feel comfy and warm. Every time I watch this show it's like I'm living the story with the characters; it's like I'm part of the Adams Foster family.

I found the show just a while ago, but it feels like it's part of my life since I was born. This show helped me make virtual friends. I don't even know if I will meet them one day, but they are like my family. This show made me change my mind about having a family. I just want to have kids and be a great mom like Stef and Lena.

Every part of this show has something special because of you: producers, actors, writers, crew, and everyone involved. You do it with your heart and the public can feel it. I just feel my heart get full when someone starts talking about The Fosters with me. I could talk about this show for hours and not even get tired.

So, I could not be more thankful for everyone that makes this show happen. You make my life complete in so many ways that I can't even explain. Thank you, thank you, thank you, thank you for being part of my life.

— Rafaela Castro

@Kathleen_Adele

Honestly, where do I even begin with The Fosters?
When The Fosters first premiered in 2013, I was just finishing my freshman year of high school. That year had proven to be one of the most difficult years of my life. I had lost my dad in 2012 and was suffering from such a

strong wave of depression. I never thought anything could come along and make me smile.

That summer, I was at a friend's house and she mentioned that the show was good and that I should check it out. It was about two episodes into the first season, so I went home and watched it.

I immediately fell in love. I can't even describe to you the amount of happiness this seemingly small thing gave me, even if it was just for an hour each week. As time went on, leading into season 1B, I found my way to what would be known as "the fandom." I didn't really understand Twitter at the time, but all I saw were tons of other people brought together by the same show, and I loved it. It also gave me a chance to follow the cast and crew, and I was blown away by just how nice, real, and humble they all were.

I was lucky enough to make so many friends through twitter and this show that I would have never met otherwise. I talk to these people every day and have even gotten to meet some of them in person. It's so crazy to know that, without this show, I wouldn't know these people who have become so incredibly important to me.

The summer of 2014, I remember seeing writer Megan Lynn's super funny and witty tweets. It wasn't long until we were following each other, sharing funny reaction photos and just chatting in general. However, she has continuously outdone herself and proven to be one of the best people in the world.

In 2016, I traveled to Los Angeles to visit Taylor (Elphaba_Anne), who I met through Twitter. Megan was so amazing to invite us both to go to the set and watch them film. Even though it was her day off, she met us at Warner Brothers, showed us around the sets, then drove us almost an hour to Long Beach. (That LA traffic was a killer).

I will never get over just how perfect and amazing that day was. I was able to hug two women who continue to inspire me every single day and prove to be the most beautiful and amazing people inside and out. Sherri and Teri were so incredibly sweet and made me feel so special.

I am forever so grateful to have met two people that helped me through such a difficult time in my life and still continue to help me. After that day, Sherri messaged me, ending the message with "be brave and bold." My sister and I were planning tattoos together, and while hers was going to say, "time makes you bolder," I wanted mine to say "be brave and bold" — a reminder I need every day suffering with intense anxiety. Sherri, being the amazing person that she is, wrote it out for me and sent me a picture. I am so excited to have something that means so much to me on my body. So, Teri and Sherri, this is a huge thank you to you. I know that it may have not seemed like much to you, but I will treasure that day for the rest of my life.

I then traveled back to Los Angeles in the summer of 2017 after visiting my brother in San Diego. Megan, being the most amazing and wonderful person, again invited us back to set. We were able to watch them film a number of scenes while sitting with other writers of the show and Bradley Bredeweg (who is also the best and will get a spotlight soon). It was so surreal to be able to be a part of that. That day, I was lucky enough to meet Cierra, who was one of the nicest (and tiniest) people I have ever met. She was so sweet and was rockin those heels until they got stuck on the backyard set. Thank you, Cierra, for being so great and as sweet in person as you are on twitter. I feel blessed to have been in the presence of such a queen.

I also got to spend a lot of time with Megan's husband and fellow writer Wade Solomon. It was so great to finally meet him and spend literally 8 hours together at video village. Also, a huge shoutout for driving us off the lot and dropping us off at the corner in a very non-sketchy way!

Again, I could never thank Megan again for being so selfless and giving us the opportunities of a lifetime. I am so grateful to have someone like her in my life, and it's so crazy that I wouldn't know this amazing person existed without this show. So, to Megan Lynn, here's a big, crazy thank you for being the absolute best always. So much love for you!

Bradley Bredeweg is also someone that deserves a round of applause. Every time I've met him, he has been so kind and so funny, and I could only aspire to be half the person that he is one day. The way he stands up for what he believes in and for what he cares about is amazing, and his dedication and love for every single one of his projects is so beautiful. I've been lucky enough to see two of his musicals: Romeo and Juliet (shoutout to my girl Ashley Argota) and The Last Breakfast Club. Both of them blew me away and watching how proud Bradley was each time was the cutest thing.

So, to Bradley: thank you for creating a show that means so much to me. Peter Paige and Joanna Johnson of course go along with this. I met Peter while he was directing the finale of season 4A, and let me just say, this man is crazy talented. Even though he was super busy, he still stopped to say hello and take a photo. Joanna I met very briefly, but she is one of the coolest people ever, and I hope to be like her one day, too.

The show in and of itself has done so much for me over the years. Like I said, when I was suffering with the worst depression of my life, I truly thought that there was never going to be anything that could come along and bring me any joy. I know it sounds crazy, but just losing myself in this show and its stories every week was exactly what I needed. It made me excited to watch every week and watching the way the characters acted together made me so incredibly happy.

As time went on, I found myself getting out of the rut that I was stuck in, and I realized The Fosters was that small spark I needed to hoist myself up. It's so crazy to think about where I might be without this little (but also very big and important) show.

As far as favorite episodes go, Padre will forever hold such a special place in my heart. Not only does it feature my favorite family relationship (Stef and Callie forever), but the words in their scene resonated with me in a way I never thought a show could do. By the time Padre aired, it had been about two years since my father's passing. I still struggled with him being gone and how to live life without him. The words that Stef told Callie in that scene nearly had me in tears. I felt like Callie, like a whole weight had been lifted off my shoulders, and to this day, think that I heard those words at the very right time in my life.

As for storylines, it's hard to choose just one. I am so grateful for a show that chooses to tackle the topics that many others tend to stray away from. However, if I had to choose just one, I would choose the one about Callie fighting against Justina and privatized foster care. That was something I never knew about, and it angered me in the way I think it was supposed to. It has made me hope to one day be able to help and do something to stop such an awful and terrible thing.

But then again, the school storyline was also one of my favorites. "Education is a right, not just for the rich and white" is so, so important, and the timing was incredible.

I am so excited to see where it goes. Like I said though, I love them all (except Brallie, but that's okay), and I am so lucky to be invested in a show that actually teaches me something new almost every episode.

I guess what I'm trying to say in this whole thing is that The Fosters has been so much more than just a show. It has been a light in the darkness and one of the best things to ever happen to me. It's so crazy to me that when this show started, I was a freshman in high school, struggling and not even seeing a future for myself. I am now a sophomore in college studying public relations and going to therapy every week to make sure that I *do* have a future. Like I said before, I don't know if things would be like this if I didn't get that spark I needed when this show came out. I am so grateful to love a show with such an important message and such great people involved.

To the cast and crew, I love you all so much, and feel like I could never thank you enough for just doing your jobs every single day. You are all such a blessing to the world, and once this show comes to an end, I am so excited to see where you go next. Thank you so much to every single one of you for sharing your talents with us and giving me something so, so important. I truly love you and this show with my whole heart and am so glad that it has been such a large part of my life. Much love.

— Kathleen Craven

@KeeffeSheena

I first heard about the show when I was reading an article about Grey's Anatomy. Up until then, I had never heard about the show. To this day, I am grateful that I did, and I always will be.

I have always felt that a show with two moms at the head was never properly addressed or explored on any TV show in the past. What attracted me to it was because it showed a family can be made up in different ways and include biological, foster, and adopted kids. I feel like I connected to the show because it raises awareness about real-life issues and the ups and downs that a family can go through in life.

To the team at The Fosters: I will always be grateful and hugely thankful to you for creating and producing a show that I hold in very high regard. In my opinion, the show does well making the family look and feel real. The relationship the moms (Teri Polo and Sherri Saum) have is one of best and most realistic portrayals of a same sex relationship that I have ever seen on any TV show. Both Teri and Sherri make it look so effortless and is a real joy to watch.

Throughout the show, the characters of Stef and Lena have taught me that love is profound and knows no boundaries. The Fosters has given me a good lesson in that it is okay to be who you are and that your family can love you and celebrate who you are.

The character I relate to most would have to be Callie (Maia Mitchell). I feel connected to her because I have always been less confident in who I am. However, watching the show has given me more confidence, and I am not as shy as I was before. She has taught me that if you work hard and follow your dreams, you can achieve them.

My favourite tweets would have to be from Bradley Bredeweg. All the pictures he sends on his twitter page showing us fans what we expect from season to season are amazing. I also like all the tweets that Sherri shares about her friendship with Teri. I love that quote from Season 1 when Stef says the line, "At end of the day, who I love shouldn't be an issue for you or anybody else. It is one of my favourite quotes from the show, and I love the fact Teri Polo has it on her Twitter page.

I would like all the team at The Fosters to know that words can't describe all the gratitude and love I have for all of them. I have learned so much and gained so much confidence through you all. I owe a big thank you to Peter, Bradley and Joanna for creating and producing the best show ever. It has really changed my life, and I am a better person because of it. I now have a lot more respect and love for our LGBTQ community and totally support same sex marriage.

— Sheena O'Keeffe

@KNwestcoast

The Fosters quite literally changed my life. It normalized a unique family and displayed a loving relationship between two middle-aged women. The Mamas fulfilled a need for me as a gay woman to see myself, also a middle-aged women, reflected in a relationship.

I actually had missed the first season of the show, but binge watched after seeing Teri Polo and Sherri Saum on a talk show. Although they were straight women, their interaction and chemistry intrigued me. After watching the first episode I was hooked and had the need to find out has much as I could about the show.

Enter Twitter.

I had never been on Twitter but found a group of people talking about the show with Sherri Saum and the anticipation of Teri Polo coming online soon. The experience I had with this Twitter group was incredibly rewarding. I found myself on my phone like an eager teenager, engaged nonstop with others, laugh crying in my desk chair as we discussed the show and the actors portraying the characters.

Enter Teri Polo.

Our conversations were so rousting that Teri Polo would jump in on occasion, thrilling us all. Cartoon caricatures of fans engaging with Teri were posted to delight and bait her (I'm a graphic designer) and her "Pologroupies" (a name she applauded). Coffee cups, wine glasses and miscellaneous other items were personally created and monogrammed with the beloved "Pologroupies" tag.

Enter Friendships.

The people on Twitter became close friends. I even traveled from the west coast to New York and Dallas to meet them. When on vacation in Los Angeles, Teri Polo herself met and then invited me to the set. She is an incredibly gracious person. TV fantasy became reality.

Enter Danny.

When the show started I was a lonely single woman, but with the encouragement of my Twitter friends I put myself out there and met a wonderful woman named Danny. We were married in Maui on October 13th. NONE of this would have happen without airing of The Fosters.

Enter Today.

Unfortunately, during third season, the show changed. I think when the network changed to Freeform the focus of the show changed to lives of the children and downplayed the relationship of the Mamas. It became a fast-paced teenage soap opera with too many storylines and characters. The compelling, evolving story of a family depicted in the first season was lost and the beautiful relationship of Stef and Lena virtually dismissed. I think the network miscalculated the huge middle-aged following and developed the series into something it wasn't meant to be. Its unique quality was turned into a lesser mainstream copycat. I miss, miss, miss the old show and the lovely characters that were presented in the pilot but will be eternally grateful for its creation.

— Kathleen Nelson

@Kristenkelso23

Dear cast, crew, and creators: my name is Kristen Kelso. I am 24 and live in Columbus, Ohio. The Fosters has changed my life in so many ways. When I first learned about the show, I was just changing channels and stopped on the promo. It looked so interesting, and I was hooked from the beginning.

The one thing that really attracted me to the show was the love of the family. I love how different it was from any other show. You really didn't see a family raised by two moms portrayed on TV. The character that I really connected with was Callie because I'm also headstrong, independent, and put the needs of others ahead of myself, which is what I love about her!

There are so many storylines that I loved, so I really can't choose a favorite. But the one that I related to the most was when Jude came out. I had just recently come out to my family. I always cared what they would think about me, but this show changed all that. I realized that I shouldn't care what others think about me and that who I love shouldn't be an issue for you or anyone else. (Which has to be my favorite Fosters quote!)

Not going to lie, my favorite episode is any episode with Brallie. I love them and hope to see them together in the end. ;)

Because of The Fosters I have met so many people who I can be myself around. Whatever I'm going through, I can always count on them to get me through it. So, thank you again for bringing this amazing show into my life. To the cast: you have no idea what your likes and replies and your tweets mean to us.

— Kristen Kelso

@leslierogers200

The Fosters is such a very important show to me. I've learned a lot in the two and a half years since I started watching. The way I found out about the show was when I was looking for a new show to watch. I came across The Fosters on a list on the internet, started watching, and never stopped.

I immediately started telling my friends and family about this show. I actually convinced my sister, mom, and best friend to watch it, and they liked it a lot. Like I was saying, The Fosters has showed me a lot, I've learned about the foster system, adoption, and so much more. I'm extremely grateful this type of show exists on TV because it breaks barriers. They show topics that many TV shows are afraid to expose. I love The Fosters so much!

— Leslie Rogers

@liarsxsab

I started watching the show because my internet best friend recommended it to me. I saw the first episode and noticed that Maia Mitchell was in the series. She has always been one of my favorite actresses.

I saw the episode where Jude arrived, and I was completely in love with his character. Jude is my favorite along with Mariana. Jude changed a lot during the series and grew up. His attitude changed, and he became more rebellious. I identified with that because I also grew and changed a lot.

Mariana is my favorite because she is an icon in every sense. She is pescatarian, feminist, and a fighter. She fights for her rights and for what she believes, and I am encouraged to inform myself and become a feminist to fight for what I believe in.

I love that the series talks about transgender people and everything they suffer. Cole and Aaron suffered a lot to be accepted, and I love that Callie defends them and makes people around them understand them. I believe that each character is unique. Lena and Stef managed to get married and did not feel afraid of what society could say, Lena and Stef both educate their children and explain everything they need. Lena put her work at risk more than once in order to teach children about necessary things.

Undoubtedly what I'm going to miss most about The Fosters is seeing the whole cast together. They look so happy being on set, and I'm really going to miss that. However, I'm also going to miss seeing a series that talks about such important issues like homophobia, racism, transphobia, and undocumented immigrants in addition to other issues that are very important for adolescents.

This series is very important for me, and thanks to it I met actors who are very important to me like Hayden and Cierra. I did not know them before, and now they are my examples to follow. I cannot reach the words to say thank you for this show because it literally changed my life. So, thanks, thanks, and more thanks.

— Martina Bruhn

@LisaHunter14 / @Roberts_Wish

The Fosters has completely changed my life in the last three years. I first came to know about the show from a dear friend. Robert had experienced significant discrimination and rejection after coming out. He found clips of the show on YouTube, and these made the world of difference to him. The positive messages, relevant and true to life portrayals, and incredible love shown in these clips became Robert's lifeline. They helped him feel less alone, more hopeful, and gave him comfort.

Unfortunately, due to a significant event, Robert took his own life, but before this he wrote a letter telling me about The Fosters, the impact it had on him, and asking me to find a way to help people struggling to feel less alone. Following this, I started watching the show and following it on social media.

Through the social media channels, I started mentoring different people and supporting them through different challenges. I met Teri, Sherri and Peter Paige at various events in LA and started building a nonprofit aimed at supporting youth, with Robert's last wish in mind and inspired by the support and encouragement from Teri and Sherri. Robert's Wish is in the latter stages of development, and we hope to launch soon. Thanks to The Fosters I have found my passion, met the most brave and incredible people and learned a lot.

It is simple: The Fosters makes a difference to so many of all ages. It covers relevant, sensitive topics in a real and powerful way. Love, equality and real life are common themes that are woven through every episode. The passion of the cast and crew shows through in every episode.

I have a great deal of respect for The Fosters team. Personally, Teri's HRC acceptance speech had a notable impact on me. It is still something I watch when I experience some difficulties and need motivation.

When I first mentioned that I was thinking about doing something in Robert's memory, both Teri and Sherri encouraged me and told me to do it. Now here I am, about to launch an online support community for youth who are being bullied or experiencing different challenges. The Fosters has played a huge part in making this a reality.

— Lisa Hunter

@lisaswiftt

I guess all I can say is thank you. Thank you to The Fosters, its creators, its writers, its crew, and its cast. When I first saw the promotion for it, I was skeptical. I didn't think it'd be something I'd watch, but I decided to anyway.

I know it sounds completely dramatic, but this show changed my life. From coming out to meeting a (now) past love to making everlasting friendships, The Fosters has had the biggest impact on my life these last few years. Who knew a television show could do such a thing?

Thank you for opening the eyes of millions of viewers, always being inclusive, always promoting justice, and speaking out about what's right. That's something noteworthy and beautiful and I hope you all are forever praised for creating that.

But most importantly, thank you for creating the family that is The Fosters Fandom. Never in my life have I felt more accepted by a group of people, some of whom I've had the pleasure of meeting in person and some who will always be virtual close friends. That is something I can never, ever forget or replace with anything else. Sure, other shows may have more awards or longer time periods, but do they have family? In the words of Lena Adams Foster, "DNA doesn't make a family, love does." And if a show can create something like that, then in my book, it's the most successful show on television. So, thank you all for your hard work, dedication, and pure love. This may be the end of the show, but the love created is everlasting. Thank you.

Love,
— Lisa

@lisetteescobar

I first found The Fosters on Netflix. Season 1B had just hit, and I was sold. The characters were so real, and the stories were nothing I'd ever seen on TV. Honestly, I still don't see any of these storylines on TV. The Fosters is breaking boundaries and bringing up topics everyone else makes too taboo to talk about.

Every character is different, and every story is different. There's a storyline for everyone to relate to. The character I relate most to is Mariana. She's the sassy, smart mouth, know-it-all, but her heart is always in the right place. It's beautiful and hilarious. A line that sticks out the most is, "Why can't you be both smart and sexy?" Because honestly, why can't anyone? I think it's so important that Mariana stands her ground and said she was smart but could also be saucy. There doesn't have to be one or the other: she can be both. Also, "Bitches get things done." YES YES YES!

The family as a whole is relatable yet different. They each teach you a different lesson. Even the guest stars have the best storylines. Mike and his addictions, Sophia and mental health, Daphne and her fight to get her daughter back, Kiara running away from her foster home, Gabe and his issues, Ana overcoming addiction, Aaron being transgender, and Ximena with DACA.

This show is staying current with what is going on in the world now. People who aren't watching the news can learn what is happening around us by watching this show!

I just wanted to thank you all for this show. Saying it changed my life is an understatement. I've met the best friends I've ever had. The experience of being on set and getting to know the cast is honestly a dream come true. I'm beyond grateful for everyone and everything I've learned and continue to learn from this show. You all are making this world a better place one episode at a time. So, thank you, thank you so much for changing my life.

With so much love,
— Lisette Escobar

@LovelessSid

When I first decided to watch The Fosters, I must've been at least 12. (I am 16 now.) I stumbled across this video of a family, and what drew me in was the fact that

Jennifer Lopez was a co-producer. (I was a massive Jlo fan back then.) Then all of a sudden I realized Maia Mitchell, a girl I watched on TV for as long as I could remember on *Mortified, Trapped* and *Castaway*, was on it, so I decided to start watching.

I didn't realize when I watched that first episode how groundbreaking it truly was. I actually brought that first episode on iTunes. Then, when I got access to US Netflix years later, I remembered the show. So, I picked up at episode two (season three just finished airing when I started to watch again) and was all of a sudden in this new obsession.

I thought it was just this drama about a family. I was young and ignorant and didn't care about political stuff. But this show helped change that. It shaped me in a way. It was groundbreaking, and the characters would shine light on issues that would teach me, help me learn, and keep me from being ignorant.

Flash forward to season two and three. It is 2016 and I am 15. Jude has these storylines about being with a guy and not knowing his sexuality. All of a sudden, I am in the same boat. Him not wanting to label his sexuality was exactly the same as me. I was confused, but I found comfort in being able to relate to Jude and finally I accepted that I am attracted to guys and girls. So, I would love to thank the writers and Hayden for being a part of how I learned about sexuality.

The best thing about the show is how political it is but also the whole aspect of the Adams Foster family. The same sex marriage, the immigration storyline, the transgender characters, and so much more. TV shows forget about this stuff or choose to ignore it; The Fosters, however, does not.

This show has helped me so much, and I have so much love and compassion for the cast, the crew, and the characters.

Side note: Please, I need a bisexual character *cough* Mariana *cough.* A question I have is for Maia and Cierra (or anyone really): what is your dream storyline? And if you could make any character bi, pansexual, or gay, who would it be and why?

There are not enough words to describe how I feel about this show, so I thank everyone who has taken part of this show to make it become such an amazing, groundbreaking program.

— Sid Cross

@LoveTeriSherri

I found The Fosters thanks to a friend that told me there was a lesbian couple starring Sherri and Teri as the moms. I was immediately hooked. What attracted me to the show was the strong connection that the moms had. Even if there were struggles, they always found a way to be with each other. The real stories, the ups and downs, and the love they had for one and another was incredible.

I think I´m connected in such a strong way with this show because it's not something that you see on TV every day. This is a show that says, "Love is love no matter what. It has no labels, no one is there to judge you in any way." This show hits so many issues that others don't talk about and topics that I didn't even know about. The best thing about this show is everything. It's all beautifully created!

How could I write the ending, how would it end? Oh Snap! I would ship all the kids to universities and give the moms a huge vacation. Maybe I'd give Lena the opportunity to have a child (even if she is 40, she still can have one) and it would just be the three of them. But maybe I would end it with just Stef and Lena in a beach house far away, enjoying each other with some peace and relaxation time. (But it is just a dream lol!).

The people I connected to the most were Teri Polo and Sherri Saum being Stef and Lena. These ladies are amazing, incredible, magnificent, brilliant, gorgeous women. There are not words to describe how great they are. They are truly genuine. I could feel the love, admiration, and all the energy they have when Teri and Sherri are together in a scene looking at each other. Or even when Teri looks at Sherri. It's something so incredible.

I have learned so much thanks to Stef and Lena. I learned that communication is really important in a relationship, how to be stronger, how to be more compassionate and respectful, to never judge before you know the other person's history, to not be stubborn like Stef (LOL! True Story), to follow my dreams, and to have passion for what I believe in. I'm just so grateful for these ladies.

My Favorite tweets are all from Teri Polo, Sherri Saum, Bradley, and Peter. Those are the best. There are a few from Teri that say:

"You can't plan your happiness… SO LIVE!!! (July 25, 2016); "Be you, love as you want to be love and jump… life is meant to be lived, not feared"; and, from January 3, 2018: "It's not the end… it's the first day of the rest of our lives! It's a beautiful 10 episodes. So much heart and soul have been put into them, by the cast and crew. Let's all hold hands and do this together. Coco."

…I'm not going to settle, I'm not going to plateau… I am going to take the joy, the love, the lessons I have learned and share this with everyone I know, as I so look forward to my new journey!!! If we ALL take this gift of the last 5 years and share it… we will continue to make a difference in lives, from this day on. "You must be the change you wish to see in the world" Gandhi. Reach out and touch more lives with your stories, that's what The Fosters was here for. You're all in charge now. Always in my heart...thank you.

I don't really have a favorite storyline because they are all amazing, but if I had to choose I would say, the moms struggling with house stuff and everything else. It's hard in these times to keep up with work, kids (even more if you have five or six) and helping them also with their struggles and troubles. I would always go with huge hands up with Stef and Lena because there were eight people in my home including my parents, and wow! I don't know how they managed that.

I would like Teri Polo and Sherri Saum to know that I admire both of them so much. They both are so extremely incredible ladies. Thank you for bringing real, honest love to life. You both have raised awareness and made a difference. Thank you for the incredible friendship, for all you both gave us, and for making us FEEL all Stef's and Lena's emotions! And being amazing, kickass role models. So much love and respect for both Teri and Sherri.

My favorite scenes are the ones with the mamas. I loved both weddings, when Lena took Stef swimming, when Lena stood by the board saying she should be the principal, when Lena walked into school with a swimsuit on, and the Mother's Day brunch with them all saying how they feel about the amazing mamas!

A few notable fans are:
@Fostersonellend,
@SaumPolo1,
@Sid_Onia__,
@RaeAnnJohnsonFL,

@AdamsFostersFamily,
@StefAFoster1.

There are so many amazing Fosters Family members on Twitter that I have had the opportunity of being friends with. That's really incredible, and I thank The Fosters for that.

To end this, I would like to say this journey with The Fosters — all the creators, writers, cast, and crew members — has been a magnificent journey that I will cherish with all my heart. I'm looking forward to the next chapter for Teri Polo, Sherri Saum, Bradley Bredeweg, and Peter Paige.

Thank You.
— Liz Lorraine C

@maebae98

What The Fosters means to me is family and friendships. Thanks to The Fosters and The Fosters cast, I know what a family is. I have friends who I talk to daily on Twitter due to The Fosters show.

I found The Fosters because my mom started watching it. She told me that it had a lesbian couple with lots of kids. That was just something I needed and wanted to feel as I was being accepted in my house.

Teri,

You mean the world to me. You have become a mother figure to me through this show. It's crazy how a fictional character on a show can mean so much to someone. Through the years you have shown me nothing but love. On days where you did your five-minute fav frenzies you always noticed me, and I just had this warm sensation each time.

There was this one time I stayed up really late on a school night just to get a single reply from you because I had felt worthless and I just needed a mama sandwich from you. You had asked me what I wanted you to say and for some reason I asked for a picture of your hand and you actually sent me a picture of your hand. To this day when I feel like I need a hand to hold to get through anything I pull up your hand picture and squeeze my phone for a few minutes and it's like you're right there with me. Thank you for being such an inspirational figure to me through the show and making everything better when I'm sad.

Love always.

Sherri,

Thank you for everything you do on the show and in person. You're such a loving and caring person. You and Teri have the most beautiful kids. You guys had made me see what a family is and how people actually love. I learned to love from watching you guys on the show. When I get older and get married I want to do exactly what you guys did — foster kids because they need the same love and validation any kid needs. Plus, there are so many kids in the foster system looking for homes.

Thank you for showing me everything!

Love always,
— Mae Burke

@maiamtchls

I found The Fosters through mutual friends on Twitter who were always tweeting about it – namely Liv

(@frnakcaslte). I said I was most interested in dramas and was reassured it would be right up my street. At this time, 3B was just ending. I didn't realize how roped in I was about to become and how many life lessons I was about to learn. I needed an excuse to watch a new show and thought, '*Hey, why not?*'

I haven't looked back since.

I very much consider myself a conscientious person who tries to be aware of as much as possible, and the show taught me things I was never aware of before. What I love so much about The Fosters is that it is not scared to talk about what many other shows would not dare to touch upon, telling the stories of those who aren't heard and have less of a voice. Story lines such as Ximena's immigration, the Mamas talking about ableism, Jude discovering his sexuality, flaws in various societal systems, giving awareness to the transgender community, and equal education for all are some of the many that I am glad have been covered over the past five seasons.

I could write a book with just how many important life lessons this show teaches. At the time I discovered the show, I was questioning my sexuality. Just seeing the dynamic of Stef and Lena and how normal their lives were was definitely a large factor in me coming to terms and accepting who I am. Learning from characters that you don't need labels, but also that labels can be empowering, was very important for me. Now I can pretty much be open about my bisexuality, as it is just another aspect of me that makes me who I am.

Not only are the characters of the show amazing, but the people who portray them are just as great. I feel privileged to have found and look up to a cast and crew who fight for what's right and try to make a positive change to this world. Their presence at events such as women's rallies, educating people who may be misinformed about certain subjects and sharing causes they believe in with the world, is something that I really admire. I am proud of each and every one of them (god I sound like a Mum).

I am grateful to have had The Fosters in my life for the past two years and want to thank everyone involved for being such a great influence on my life. I wouldn't be the same person without you, and I truly wish everyone the best because they deserve it for not just touching my life, but many others, too.

— Zoe King

@marlenaNmurray1

I was sitting on the couch just minding my own business when my sister turned on this show The Fosters. My eyes were suddenly glued to the TV. My sister mentioned it was about two lesbians and asked me if I wanted to watch the show from the beginning. Of course, I said yes because I was gay, but I was afraid to let anyone know it.

I was so connected to the show when Lena sat down with Mariana and said, "DNA doesn't make a family — love does." It really touched something deep in my heart because I was abandoned by my mother at the age of nine. I just love how this show has affected so many people around us and made me feel okay to be myself.

I have so many favorite scenes from The Fosters I don't know where to start. I just adore the Stef and Lena scenes. They are my most favorite. I absolutely love each and every member of The Fosters cast and crew, but I can't lie, Teri Polo is my favorite. She inspires me so much. The first time she ever tweeted me she said, "just because I don't respond doesn't mean I don't see it coco." It just touched my heart. I love how positive she is and how she always has something nice to say. She has one of the biggest hearts. I love her.

If I could write the ending of The Fosters (even though I don't want there to ever be an ending), I would make one of the happiest scenes where the whole family was in one room laughing together and Jesus got better, Brandon got into Juilliard and became a pianist, Lena became principal of Anchor Beach, Callie found out what she truly wanted to become and went through with it, Mariana got accepted to a great college and became a cheerleader, Jude found the love of his life, and Stef already has everything she ever dreamed of — a loving happy family with a beautiful wife — and they all lived happily ever after :)

— Marlena Murray

@maryjo777

Hi! My name is Mary Anne Collins. I'm originally from Scotland now living in Canada. I love this show so much. It covers pretty much everything I have been through in my life so far.

I was a foster kid from the age of 7 to 18. I never found my forever family — I guess that a part of me is still looking. What I love about this show more than any other is that it covers real circumstances that happen to foster kids that other shows don't cover.

I truly wish that this show continues to bring happiness to me and so many other people worldwide. I love all the cast members, especially the mums as they hold everyone together even when the worst curve balls of life strike.

A massive thank you to everyone involved in the making of this wonderful show, from the directors, producers, writers, and the whole cast. No matter what role you play, you are all amazing!

Lots of love and gratitude.

P.S: if there is ever a role for a Scottish woman in the future, I would be more than happy to help out hahaha.

— Maryanne Collins

@Me_ohmaia

Why do I love The Fosters, you ask? What's not to love! This show has given me the best 4+ years I could ever ask for. This show has been an escape. Each week for just one hour I get to forget about my worries and just enjoy the trials and ups and downs of this family.

They are a fictional family, but their stories are so true and real. When you look into each and every one of these characters, you are bound to find yourself. I see myself in Stef, Mariana and Callie. I'm headstrong, full of sass and am always putting others before myself.

Family is so important to me, and I would be completely lost without mine. Over the last 4+ years the Fosters have also become my family, and I would be lost without them. This show is more than a show. This show leaves no rock unturned. No topic undiscussed. They talk about every topic, whether it be taboo or not. They also somehow always manage to be up with the news and current events happening in the world, which is another reason why this show is so relatable.

Teens and young adults can look to this show to learn valuable life lessons. The Fosters also brings to light issues that one may never experience firsthand, such as transgender teens coming out to their parents and having them not accept you or coming out to your parents that you are gay. It educates people on all matters.

This show also teaches us that DNA doesn't make a family, love does. This message is so powerful and one that I will always remember. Another reason why I love this show is because everyone has a place. They exclude no one, and everyone matters. Everyone is worth saving and no one is disposable.

This show has truly changed my life. I have made life-long friends because of this show and for that I am forever grateful. They will forever be by my side, and I have this show to thank for that. I have also been blessed to have met the cast and creators of the show. They have all welcomed me with open arms and are truly the nicest people ever.

When I say this show has the best cast and crew, that is an understatement. These people are incredible and truly care about their fans. We aren't just fans, we are family. Being able to visit the set of The Fosters is something that I will never forget. It truly is a unique and exciting experience every time.

Maia Mitchell, you have been someone that I've looked up to for the past four years. Your endless amount of facial expressions and gifs have gotten me through some rough days. You've made me smile even when I didn't think I could. Thank you for being you!

Cierra Ramirez, you are a little ray of sunshine. You are so warm and bubbly and honestly just a joy to be around. Any time that I get to be around you, you make me a happier person. Your light is contagious, so keep on shining.

Hayden Byerly, you my friend are hilarious. You never fail to make me laugh and you continue to surprise me with your vast knowledge on basically everything. It's an honor to call you my friend.

David Lambert, you are a sweet soul. You are so kind and have such a warm and genuine smile. You inspire me every day to be more giving of myself. And let's not forget your legendary hiatus beard!

Noah Centineo, you are just a ball of energy with so much wisdom to give. I swear your tweets need to be put into a book. You are so passionate and full of such great insight.

Tom Williamson, your smile lights up a room, and you are so genuine. You have left a lasting impact on my life with your optimism and cheerful attitude. You inspire me every day.

Bradley Bredeweg, you are a man of many talents. You are so talented, and I am so blessed to have attended two of your plays. You are such a kind man with a big heart, and it's an honor to know you.

Maia Mitchell, Cierra Ramirez, Hayden Byerly, David Lambert, Noah Centineo, Sherri Saum, Teri Polo, Danny Nucci, Tom Williamson, Bradley Bredeweg, and Peter Paige: I want to thank you from the bottom of my heart (or the top, whichever one means more.) You have all taken the time to chat with me during my visits on set which means the world to me. I will always hold those memories close to my heart.

Also, a major shout out to the best crew around. Your efforts and work do not go unnoticed. Thank you! This show is more than what meets the eye. There is so much depth and truth poured into each episode. There are still so many stories that need to be told, and I cannot wait to watch this family grow for years to come.

Everyone needs to be watching this show. It is for the people. It teaches us valuable lessons, and the world needs it. I need it! I will never be able to thank you enough for this show or tell you how much it truly means to me, but I hope that this letter gives you at least a glimpse into how much this show and you all mean to me.

Your friend,
— Maddy Salthouse

@MHadamsfoster

I first found The Fosters when I was watching ABC Family and the preview came on. From the first time I saw it, I was anxious to see the show. The original episode had me feeling a way I never felt before watching something. It was so powerful and meaningful.

My favorite scene was when Stef went to Callie and Jude's foster home and saw them hugging through the door. I also always loved Stef and Callie's storyline. This show has opened my eyes. I connected with it because it's just a family that I happened to fall in love with. I stuck with it, and I'm so happy I did! I've watched it ever since and never missed an episode. As you can see, I love this show and I love the two great women who run it: Sherri and Teri!

— Marina Makastchian

@MonicaThue

Hi! I am not the best at writing, but I do want to say a few things. I found this show one Saturday morning while drinking my coffee and flipping through On Demand. It caught my attention from the 1st scene in episode one, and I have been hooked ever since. I have recorded every show since and watch it on Netflix on my iPad whenever I am not near my television. I could not even count how many times I have watched every episode.

I kind of lived a Brady Bunch-type life growing up, as my husband would say. Had some struggles in high school dealing with an alcoholic father, but in all it was a happy life. The Fosters taught me how to really love, how to really care, how not to judge one another, and most of all, what family really means.

I had the opportunity in October of 2016 to meet and have lunch with Teri Polo. I had a great conversation with her. I had been a big fan of hers for a long time and got to see the real her. Teri is a great actress, but most of all she is the most caring, compassionate loving person I have met. Her family is the most important to her, but she has treated her Foster fans and her Twitter followers just like one of her own.

I am really going to miss this show when it is over, but I want to thank the writers, the producers and the actors themselves for giving us this show, giving us something to look forward to, something to enjoy, and something to show us all what family, love and compassion really means during a time when this world seems to be a bit out of sorts.

I also want to thank them for my new Foster family and my new Twitter friends, some of who I have had the opportunity to meet and some I will hopefully meet someday.

You all are the greatest. BE PROUD BE YOURSELF. LOVE MORE, JUDGE LESS. IT'S WHERE YOU BELONG. DNA DOESN'T MAKE A FAMILY: LOVE DOES.

— Monica Thue

@monika_sch1

First my friend talked about this show. She asked me if I knew the story and I said I had heard about it. However, it wasn't until after I started watching that I realized this was something I really needed in my life. The characters are so real. The show is so real.

Teri Polo is a goddess. It was love at first sight. I wanted to watch more about this family. I started reading about them on internet, and I wanted to find a place where I could talk with other fans or just read what was happening with the actors in real life. My absolute favorite character is Stef because she is so strong, smart, loves hard, and is such a lovable person. I really love her. And I wanted to know her in real life, too. I wrote a letter to Teri and sent it to her. I wanted her to know how I feel when I see her or just hear her voice.

I really love the chemistry that Teri has with Sherri Saum. They are in love with each other...and that is what I want in my own life. My favorite scenes were their weddings because it was like: finally. I was crying a lot because it was so beautiful, and I felt like real love could really happen. Teri is the best woman in the whole world. She has a really good sense of humour, and she can make me smile just by being who she is. She is the most beautiful girl in the whole world.

— Mónika Schnierer

@Nakb21

Hi! What awesome tribute for The Fosters! Beautiful. I am Dutch, so I understand and speak English very well, but writing it down is difficult. So, it is hard for me to explain what I feel and think about The Fosters.

The show is awesome, and I ship Stef and Lena. Before The Fosters, I was already a fan of Teri Polo. Now she is acting with Sherri, and I think they are the best TV couple! So natural. The show deserves a lot more viewers! In 2015, I was on a holiday in LA and I had the honour to meet Bradley. I admire him. So nice and talented. I was at WB, but I did not see T/S. But it was great.

— Neely Karel

@natymerlo2

Hi Teri! I'm Natalia from Argentina, and I'm here to THANK YOU. It was right after watching your acting on The Fosters that I decided to get out of the closet and tell my mother I'm a 29-year-old bisexual girl. Specifically, the episode in which Frank dies. Thank you for being such a great actress and making me feel the way the character must have felt at the moment. So, I told her, and everything went great. She loves me all the same, no matter what.

THANKS again. Lots of love! Thanks for being an amazing Stef.

— Natalia Merlo

@Ncosenti

Hi! I would like to say that this cast has helped me through so much. It has taught me about love, compassion, and what being a family is. The character on The Fosters that has influenced me the most is Brandon. He is always taking care of those in need and is there for his family and others. I love The Fosters cast so much.

This show has taught me so much — the whole cast has. I love The Fosters so much!

— Nicole Marie Cosentino

@njhvoguex

I found out about The Fosters after hearing a few of my friends talk about the show. Ever since, I have been watching the show every week!

Just this past summer of 2017, I managed to get my parents to start watching the weekly episodes. We all look forward to spending this time together and this has helped us bond! I love how The Fosters is such a realistic show and how they are aired so timely. For example, the situation the country is in with DACA and how the Fosters brought that to light.

My two favourite characters are Mariana and Callie. Mariana is such an independent woman and knows how to get what she wants. Yet, like a normal teenager, she has vulnerabilities. I really feel for Callie, and all the tough luck she has had throughout her life in foster care. Now that she is with the Fosters, I can really see how much her character has grown and adapted! It's beautiful.

I can connect with the character Jesus the most. His TBI really affects him in many ways, including with learning. I can relate to this because I also have a learning disability and have had an IEP my whole life in school.

I love all of the cast members. They all seem to have such close relationship and bond with one another! I watched both Teen Beach Movie 1 and 2, which Maia Mitchell starred in. Teen Beach was one of my favourite movies, and she did a wonderful job! I love British and Australians (+their accents), so go Maia!

Cierra Ramirez is such a talented actress and singer! Her Discreet EP I had on repeat for quite a while! Love her voice, and I hope I can see her perform live sometime! She's also so talented at portraying the character Mariana.

Hayden Byerly. He is younger than me yet look where he is in his life! He acts way more maturely than me. And he started his acting career so young, and I know he will really go places! Kudos to him!

— Lauren Watt

@northhillchris

How did I discover The Fosters? I had read some advanced publicity about a new show featuring two lesbian moms and a family of foster, adopted and biological children. I was waiting for it to come on, and I've been watching from the first episode. I have never been disappointed (although I have often been greedy and wanted more "Mom" time on screen).

It was the first time I'd seen a real-life family headed by two loving characters who just happened to be women. I can relate to them, because they are me. Stef and Lena represent a true marriage regardless of what sex they are, a marriage that has its ups and downs and trials but continues because there is true and deep love between them.

How happy I was to see the actresses Teri Polo and Sherri Saum develop a real friendship through their characters and share that with their fans — a friendship that I'm certain will last the rest of their lives. You can see it as they introduced each other at the Human Rights Campaign ceremonies honoring each of them. I think true Fosters fans realize that the entire cast has a love for one another in real life that absolutely pours through their performances.

Favorite episodes? How can I pick? There have been so many for so many different reasons. I love the weddings, both of them. Although I hated Stef getting cancer, I loved how the couple dealt with it. I loved the camping trip. Favorite scenes are many as well. Some of them include Lena helping Jude wipe off his nail polish and explaining how he should never be ashamed of who he is. Lena telling Mariana never to play small for anyone (you are already really short!), Stef telling her father not to come to the wedding unless he was 100% behind who she was...and Stef talking to the late Frank in the car as he sends a message with the snowflakes in San Diego. Lena talking to the Ghost when Jesus was in critical condition was brilliantly written and acted.

I want the cast to know just how much the show has meant to me, how it made me feel warm and loved just knowing someone understands who gay people really are, and how I will always remember what a good show it is.

Thank you to the cast and producers.

— Chris Caccamo

@okaychyler

Dear Fosters Cast and Crew,

Hi! My name is Catthy, and I'm 16 years old. I first found out about The Fosters through a friend of mine. She constantly recommended it to me, and I decided to start it last year. I ended up binging all the way up to the finale of 5A in just a week.

I'm not normally the kind of person to binge TV shows at all, to be honest. Plus, it's my junior year of high school, so I wouldn't have lots of time to spare. But I easily made time for The Fosters. It's such an amazing show, and I can't believe I didn't start it earlier. Every episode keeps me on my feet.

On top of that, The Fosters is so much more. It stands for so many important things and brings up topics that other TV shows would be afraid to even touch. It is the prime example of what TV shows should be using their media outreach for. I'm really interested in film and television production, and one day, I truly hope to be a part of something as amazing as what the Fosters is doing.

One of my favorite things about the show is that two lesbian moms are the parents. We never see any TV shows centered around two moms raising a family and personally, for me, a closeted gay, it really meant a lot to me to see all aspects of Stef and Lena's relationship on TV and the representation it provides.

The role that the cast plays off-screen in advocating LGBT representation, especially Sherri and Teri, has changed my life as well. I am lucky to be able to have them to look up to, as they taught me to accept myself more in my own skin, and I'm forever grateful.

So again, thank you SO MUCH to the cast and crew that have made The Fosters what it is.

— Catthy

@PinkUnicornes

Hello, The Fosters cast!

My name is Julie, and your show made me stronger. Jude made me proud of who I am as a lesbian. I was bullied for it, but The Fosters makes me stronger! I was in foster homes for five years, and this show makes me stronger! I love you all and thank you from all my heart.

— Ju Mezonniaud Picat

@pnkluv07

I found The Fosters because one day I was flipping through the channels and I saw the promo on ABC Family. I got interested seeing that. What attracted me to the show was the family aspect of it. Not many shows focus on family these days.

I feel connected because I feel different every day and I'm not sure why. But this show just makes my life...normal, I guess? The best things about the show is they go over so many important topics like rape, DACA, foster systems, the LGBTQA+ community, etc.

If I could write the ending, I would write one where the only important relationship is the family. The endgames would be Stef/Lena, Jonnor, Matiana, Jemma, and I don't know about Brallie. I love them together, but I love them more as friends. I'd definitely give them friendship scenes. If I don't have romantic Brallie, I'd have

Brandon with Grace and single Callie because she needs her own time.

I connect with all the characters in the show. Maybe Brandon because he does so much to care for everyone, but they don't realize it. Callie and Mariana probably influence my life the most because Callie is so determined to help others and Mariana is all about girl-power.

I can't pick just one storyline as my favorite. Most of the storylines are my favorites because they're important AND entertaining. My favorite scenes are all the Brallie scenes (except their arguments), the Jonnor kiss/pinkie holding, Brandon treating Grace like a princess, any parent/child scenes, or anything that is cute and/or brings a smile to my face.

— Jen Johnson

@pxggyrogers

Dear Teri and Sherri,

Hi, you two! First of all, let me just apologize for doing the lazy thing and typing this letter. I would handwrite, but I would not want to risk the embarrassment of you not being able to read it. So, I'll just jump right into it.

October 2013. No, don't worry, I don't have the initial pilot date wrong. This was the month I went to Florida with my family (I'm all the way across the pond in the UK), and this is where I saw a poster for The Fosters. A few different things caught my eye.

I got home two weeks later and the first thing I did was look the show up. I read the plot and it all seemed interesting to me. Kids being raised by two mums was certainly something I had not heard of yet or even seen apart from the odd cameo on the odd TV show, but I feel that doesn't count as good representation.

I went on from then not knowing exactly what to expect, but now all I can say is thank god that 14-year-old me had a curious mind. Because this show has truly, *truly* changed me for the better.

I've always been different. In both my family and social life, I am what my family calls 'a sensitive soul' and often prefer to do things on my own, my own way. Not that there is anything particularly wrong with that, but when I reached high school, after being teased in little school,

I went in with zero self-confidence and a whole lot of anxiety. I felt like I couldn't trust anyone who wanted to be my friend because it would end up being some kind of joke. I still don't know how my brain had gotten to this mindset, but it just did.

Even though my high school experience turned out to be a good one, I was still stuck with crippling anxiety. I found this show, and I was actually quite overwhelmed by how much I suddenly felt at home with these characters. As crazy as it may sound, Stef and Lena make me feel safe. When Stef says to Callie, "You're not disposable" it really struck me because, like Callie, I really needed to hear that from the point I was in at that time of my life.

The Fosters let me know and helped me to know that whatever happens it will be okay. There will always be a place to call home and there will always be a place to be accepted.

The two of you have brought me so much joy over the past years, watching your interviews both separately and together. The love and support you show your fans has sometimes been the main thing that has gotten me through the day. If I was ever feeling shitty, I would go watch you guys, whether it was in a new video or one that I had seen a hundred time over. They always made me smile and laugh, ultimately putting me in a better mood, and that I couldn't ever thank you enough for.

I am from Manchester. I had to wake up last year to not only find out that my home has been attacked, but also that one of my best friends died in the terror attack at the Ariana Grande concert. It sent me back to square one — at least I felt it did — with my depression and anxiety of leaving my home.

But then the show returned. I had been counting down the days for the show to come back because, even though I of course knew I had my family's support, I needed and want my Foster family back on my screen. You guys helped me through all the tough times I've faced, and every episode teaches me something and gives me something to make me feel better. The show has carried me through the dark times I've been having.

Watching episodes where Stef loses her father and when Lena loses the baby, watching both characters pull through their grief and tragedies helped me comprehend with my own. I *truly* can't express how much this show helps me. Already it is making me feel less alone than I have been feeling this past month and a half. Stef and Lena have showed me over the years that it's okay not to be okay at times. What I have to make sure to do is to know when to tell someone instead of keeping it to myself and going down the spiral of depression that I have only just gotten out of a few years back.

All I ever wish for is to hug you both so tight and just thank you for everything you have done for me because you have done so much. You've made me feel less alone, you've pulled me through hard times, and you've made me feel that things will be okay even when it doesn't feel like it. You showed me that no matter who you are, you are valid, and you are special in your own way. Unfortunately, living over here in the UK makes the possibility of meeting you a whole lot harder. But from all the way over here I still feel your love by the messages you give out.

So, to round up my long venting. I will just say once again, thank you so much for everything you have done for me. For how much you've helped. I will never be able to thank you enough. This show is everything to me and will truly always be a part of me. I will be eternally grateful for this show helping shape me into the person I am now.

I consider myself lucky to have found this show because I don't know where I would be without it, with it helping me through my anxiety and depression. Without it I'm not sure what kind of person I would be today, and without you two inspiring me every day I am not sure where I'd be.

I love you both so much. You make me so happy and help me get through the day when I'm having a tough time. I made it through my exams with all the strength I had and now I am a student of TV and Radio in University. And if I didn't have inspirations like you, I don't think I would have had the motivation and inspiration to push through.

Thank you both. You're amazing and such beautiful women. I hope this letter gets to you, so you can see how much you do.

(If I had written this by hand, there would have been some serious tear stains on the paper. My god, what are you two doing to me?!)

All my love,
— Rebecca McMorrow

@queenmaiamitch/@hudzxo

Words can't describe how much The Fosters meant to me. It helped me during a really hard time in high school when I felt alone. The friends I met through watching the show helped me cope — it made me feel like I had another family. The lessons I've learned from this diverse and inclusive show helped guide me through my adolescence. I have grown up with the show, and now I'm pursuing university with an open mind and confident soul because I've learned so much from the experiences and people who have shaped me during my time in The Fosters fandom. I'm sure the legacy The Fosters has left on Freeform will not go unnoticed, and forever more I will be grateful for what this show has offered me. Thank you, truly.

— Huda

@RaeAnnJohnsonFL

There is nothing I could write that would be worthy enough of the tribute each of you deserve. The inclusiveness you have shown with your storytelling has only been matched by your openness and inviting dialogue with fans. It didn't go unnoticed the way each of you poured your heart into your art for 104 episodes to collaboratively create this masterpiece known as The Fosters.

The Fosters represents the most relevant and current content while simultaneously being ahead of its time. This show is a trailblazer with storylines that resemble headlines to the point that the writers seem to be clairvoyant.

The most undervalued part of this show, in my opinion, has always been the casting. Deb George and that department assembled the most familial and realistic ensemble of actors to play the Adams Foster family. The friendships that have ensued are a testament to the casting department's proficiency.

Thank you to the writers for creating scripts that made us feel. You even achieved the art of making us feel a particular emotion one week and then making us feel the exact opposite emotion the following week about a particular subject. A special thank you to Wade, Kris, and Megan for being so interactive with the fans and writing tweets when you weren't writing scripts.

There is so much appreciation for the producers and creators of this show for conceptualizing this story, being passionate about their vision, bringing it to fruition and then into our homes each week. The way the stories were written, acted, and directed created an unparalleled connection between the viewer and the characters.

Teri, Sherri, David, Maia, Cierra, Noah, Hayden, Danny, and Annika were so on top of their craft and believable as their respective characters which made it more like going home to see our family than watching a television show each week. It is not uncommon to hear fans say they'd "die without" their favorite show. However, The Fosters has fans that have commonly said, "this show saved my life." There is a profound difference in these two statements. You all played fictional characters that help people find their real truth and literally saved lives...what greater feat is there?

Sherri is undoubtedly the MVP for live tweeting more times and from more time zones than anyone else over these past 5 years. I tweeted once that I felt the need to disclose my Sherri bias at the beginning of every conversation, and that was probably the most honest, least sarcastic thing I have ever tweeted.

Sherri, I want you to know that every live tweet, every response, every like, every RT, every photo, and every moment of your time was appreciated and will continue to be treasured. Your generosity has been humbling beyond words. I've witnessed your small acts of kindness and large philanthropic gestures and am equally impressed by both. You parent so many more souls than your boys. You teach others, by your words and by your example, to be better and to want to be better. You have given many fans, some for the first time in their lives, a role model to emulate. Your heart is so big and far reaching — the lives you have touched can never be untouched. It is only the most special of people that are entrusted with parenting the masses, and you are one of them.

With love and respect,
— Rae Ann Johnson

@RealLove4ever3

My name is Marquita Robinson. I love the show, and I first found it through Netflix. I saw two diverse women together and a diverse family and that immediately attracted me to the show. I think I connected in such a strong way to the show because I am LGBTQA+ and I love anything about family. The best thing about the show to me is the lessons you can get from some of the situations that go on in the show and the message that no matter who you choose to love, you shouldn't feel unhappy or ashamed about it. Love is love no matter who it comes from.

The other best thing about the show is that it shows that we all have two things in common, which are the ability to love and that we are all human beings who deserve equal rights. My perfect ending for the show would be that everyone will be with who they want to be with and be happy. I would love to see Lena and Stef still together and happy. I would love to see an ending where the message is very clear on how violence and hatred towards someone for whatever reason is not the way to solve anything. I would just like to see the family love and be happy.

I think I connected to Mariana the most because she is the typical teenager I was when I was her age. I understand her feeling powerless and going to therapy about the way she was feeling.

Now the people who influenced me the most would be Stef and Lena. I love how they show that good communication skills are very important to have in a relationship. I love how they make time to reconnect with one another and try to make time to spend together.

My favorite tweet would be anything from Sherri or Teri. I would like Teri and Sherri to know that I love how in-tune they are with each other whether on or off screen...it's beautiful to see two women getting along together to me because Lord knows that can be very difficult sometimes...lol.

I would like the entire cast and crew to know that I very much appreciate seeing people being part of such important topics to those who are still fighting to be heard and respected. A favorite storyline and scene for me was when Stef and Lena...no, wait, anything with those two ladies is a favorite for me...lol.

My favorite episode is when Lena had the baby in her dream and they got to hold her together. It was a short moment but still my favorite episode because of that scene. Having children brings so much joy and laughter.

My question for everyone would be, what would they like to see happen in the real world from the show?

I would like to mention a notable fan by the name of Sherri and Teri France (@SherriTeri_FR on Twitter.) She is a very thoughtful and sweet person because she says a lot of nice things about the show, she draws pictures of the people involved in the show, and she raised money for Sherri's birthday, which I thought was very sweet of her. Thanks, and love to everyone involved.

Peace,
— Marquita Robinson

@RihIsaidit

The Fosters is notably one of my top three favorite TV shows ever. I've never loved a show so much that I really felt I knew the entire cast and crew. This show really has touched my heart in several different ways.

At first, I thought this was just a good show with a good story line. It was something different. Something new. But as I began to watch it even more I realized that it was reality. It was something more than just another show. These people really took their time to craft this show and make it real about true life.

The Fosters puts me through SO MANY EMOTIONS AND I LOVE IT! I am always on the edge of my seat! This show is truly amazing. When I think of The Fosters I think of LOVE. A show about two moms raising kids they love and adopted and guess what...the family is diverse. That's love!

Do you know how much our world needs this right now? It's full of hate and division. I watch this show because it's what I wish more of our world would realize. We need to look out for one another and love each other! You know how many kids need homes out here and how many people just need love no matter what their situation?

The Fosters goes beyond and shows just how to do it the right way. Two moms raising a family was one thing, but the diversity and love this show brings really drew me in. I could not believe how incredible this show was to me. It still brings me so many surprises, and I just can't fathom what I would do without it.

I'll tell ya, I love everyone's characters. This show has such talented actors and actresses that it makes it even better. They become the character, and they fit so well. I love the twins' chemistry. Cierra came into her character perfectly and I just love her. Noah has done such an excellent job, and I just see the talent he brings as he is able to transition. Just incredible. Jude is wonderful. I love him in every way. His character is very special to me in that he's developed so much. Callie's character is the glue to this show, and I'm always impressed in what she brings.

I'd say my favorite characters are Stef, Lena, and Mike. Mike is such a great guy. I really love his personality, and he is so helpful and thoughtful. No matter what the circumstance, he is going to try his best with a smile. I truly love that guy. Stef is absolutely amazing. Teri really gives it her all, and I can't imagine another person playing this part. Teri is so dedicated and talented that I feel her passion, and it's so believable that I sometimes start clapping and speaking to the TV when she delivers some great lines.

Stef's chemistry with Lena is pure love. The love they have for those kids just warms my heart. Lena has a very special place in my heart. Her sweet, kind heart is the balance the kids need, and I love to see her interact with the kids.

Sherri is absolutely beautiful. The moment I saw her in this show I screamed! She's beautiful inside and out, and I just feel a true connection with her. She goes hard for the show like none other. I loved how she kept the fans engaged by posing pics, tweeting, making videos, and talking with the fans. Although Sherri has a beautiful family of her own, she really dedicated a lot of her time to her job for this show on and off screen. I really can appreciate that. Thank you, Sherri!

To Bradley, Peter, Joanna, and all the writers, makeup artists, stylists, set designers, creative directors, crafty, director of photography, crew, etc.: thank you so much. I really appreciate you all. Without you and everyone working together we couldn't have witnessed such a great show. You all worked so hard and continue to work hard. Long days and hours. I am saying this because you give it your all. No matter what anyone says, outside of people whom have already been touched by this show, I want you to know The Fosters was needed. You guys did it. Thank you for never giving up. Continue to keep giving it your all cause we really do appreciate it.

Thank you, and I love you all,
— Paige Fields

@ronniesramirez

Hi, my name is Izzy (@ronniesramirez) and I'm from Houston, TX. I discovered The Fosters by seeing the commercial for the pilot on TV. I recognized Maia Mitchell and Jake T. Austin from Disney, so I thought I could check out this show when it premiered. After watching the first episode, I immediately fell in love with the show, so I kept watching every week and became OBSESSED.

The storylines and characters kept me intrigued and were so relatable. I realized how much of an impact this show was going to make on so many people watching. I would beg my friends to start watching the show. Thankfully they did and are as much in love with the show as I am.

In the beginning, I related with Maia's character Callie the most because she was the main character and I usually fall for characters who are a little troubled. However, as the show went on, Cierra's character Mariana became my favorite and is my favorite to this day. We are very similar in terms of personality and academics.

Because of this show, Cierra became one of my idols. She is so beautiful, caring, inspiring, and she loves her fans so much. I love how much she interacts with her fans, including me. Every time I get a tweet from her or she likes my tweet, I freak out. I know she knows how much I love and support her, and I'm so proud of her and all her accomplishments. I can't wait to meet her one day and give her the biggest hug and thank her for everything she's done for me.

I just want to thank the show because it has taught me so many things. It's also the reason I made a Twitter, where I made so many friends who also love The Fosters as much as I do. It's the one show we can talk about, fangirl, and relate to. If it weren't for the show, I wouldn't have met my best friend Cassie (@TeamBrallie_), who has been my best friend since 2014. We met on Twitter and we finally met IN PERSON just last year.

To conclude this long message: thank you, The Fosters, for changing my life and many other lives. Thank you for EVERYTHING.

— Izzy Choudhury

@RTrain_BNasty

Dear Teri and Sherri,

First of all, thank you for the show, and thank you for being a part of it. I'm so grateful that this show exists and feel honored to be part of this wonderful fandom. We're a small fandom, but hey, that's why it feels more like family :).

When I started watching The Fosters I was just looking for another show to watch and didn't think that this show would have such an impact on my life. I've been a fan of other shows, too, but The Fosters is something special. Since the show tackles so many social issues, I've become more of an activist. I'm ready to fight anyone who says anything racist, homophobic, transphobic, misogynistic etc.

What I especially love about the show is that they show things from different points of view and reveal things that aren't always black and white. For example, when we think about abortion, the first thing that comes to our mind is that people do it willingly, but you usually don't really think that you sometimes HAVE to get an abortion in order to not risk your own health.

The Fosters is not just a show that you watch to just enjoy and maybe forget about your own problems. The Fosters helps you learn something and makes you a better person, and in my opinion that's the best thing you can do when you create a show or sign on to be part of it.

What I've never seen anywhere else before is how much you two support the LGBTQ community. It feels like it's not just another job for you, but that it's really important to you and dear to your heart. You two have such big hearts, and you can't imagine how much you help people. I can't imagine having better role models in my life. Please never change!

The show has also helped a lot of people come out. I can't talk about such an experience because I'm not gay, but The Fosters has made me question my sexuality a lot. I don't think I'm straight, but I don't know what I am. Maybe bi? I don't know, and I feel like it's okay to not know. Sometimes I feel like I have to have this figured out, but then you see on screen that you don't have to label yourself. Or that you maybe find it out later in life.

For example: Stef. I see myself a lot in her. I don't like to talk about my emotions. I'm stubborn, and she didn't come out until her mid-twenties. The Fosters definitely helped me to see that if I fall in love with a woman, it will be okay, I will be able to have a family and it won't be any different than a heterosexual couple.

So dear Teri, thank you for portraying someone that I can easily identify with. And thank you to you and Sherri for portraying the best couple on screen. When I see Stef and Lena, I want to be part of such a wonderful, supportive and loving couple. They finally make marriage look somewhat good to me. I don't have any good role models in my family when it comes to marriage, so that's why it's nice to see a healthy marriage on screen that I can hold on to. (I mean, I don't want to get married anyway, but still it's nice to see that a marriage can actually work.)

But actually, the most beautiful thing about this show is your friendship, Teri and Sherri. I've never witnessed such a beautiful friendship, and this is the thing that makes me most happy: that you two have found each other. Just seeing your tweets, Instagram posts, interviews, etc. always make my day.

Especially during these times, it's important for people to watch The Fosters. Maybe it doesn't change other people's opinions, but at least it makes you think about certain issues. If we had more people like you in this world, then the world would be a better place.

So, thank you from the bottom of my heart. Much love from Germany,
— Melina Bongartz

@SarahaFGee

Hi, Sherri! Hi, Teri!

I don't really know how to start this, but I really need to tell you both how much you've done for me. There are no words that can ever describe how grateful and blessed I am and how I'm feeling about you both.

When my best friend Melina (@Rtrain_BNasty) told me to watch the show, I didn't expect that this show and especially you both would change my life in so many different ways.

Right before the show came out, I couldn't find a way to imagine myself happy and with my own family.

Some years ago, I had a girlfriend. I took this relationship really seriously but never saw us having our own family. It's so hard to say, but when she broke up with me I felt a little bit relieved in some ways. I didn't have to tell anyone that I was in love with a girl anymore, and I would have a family like everyone else in the future.

Can you believe that? I couldn't put it together. Two girls creating a family was so unbelievably far away for me. That's why I started dating men. It was a really horrible time, because this wasn't for me. I felt this wasn't right, but I couldn't let it go.

So finally, I started watching The Fosters, and I finally started to understand what it was all about. I don't necessarily need a man to create a family when there's enough love to share. And this was the time in which I finally could be honest to myself and be the person who I am. I really tried to change but I couldn't, and you both taught me that I never had to.

Even if I tried, I could never express how much this means to me. The feeling that you have when you think you have to decide between being the person you want to be and having a family is truly awful and made me sick.

So, thank you for just opening my eyes. It was so unbelievably refreshing to see how normal Stef and Lena's life together is, because it is.

After that I realized how I slowly changed because I started to understand what I was searching for all these years. I wasn't interested in finding love while I was dating men, and I didn't pay so much attention to it until I saw how much Stef and Lena were in love. Their love was the perfect example, which I needed to see.

Stef's storyline taught me so many more things. When I had my girlfriend, my mom wasn't amused about the whole thing, and it was really hard to know that she wouldn't support me. It was so good to see that Stef has some of these problems as well. You always feel lonely in these situations, and when I saw Stef struggling with her dad not accepting her, I felt a little bit relieved because sadly many people have those problems. Seeing how Stef breaks free out of all these boundaries gave me strength to do the same.

I found the courage to come out to myself and my friends. I don't think I'm ready to do it in front of my whole family, but I'm on a good way, and that's just because of you, Teri and Sherri. Also, I learned to call myself gay/lesbian for the first time, and you don't know how much courage you need to say it out loud for the first time. You sent me on the right way, and I will always be grateful for that.

Furthermore, I really love how Stef changed her style. I always felt I needed to dress how the society expects it from me, but I never felt comfortable about wearing clothes I didn't like that much. Stef's speech about being herself and not caring about other people and what they think about her also gave me strength to be myself. It feels unbelievably good to finally be yourself, to dress like you want to, and not have to hide anymore. Just because of you I stopped thinking about others. I don't really care about them anymore. My favorite motto is 'Live and let live'.

You don't know how proud I am to be a part of your fandom. I feel so really safe in our The Fosters community, and you both are so important for all of us. Please never forget this. Watching your interviews and hearing all your words you choose to support the LGBTQ community is just heartwarming, and I could listen to it endlessly. You both have your hearts in the right place, and I think there are so many people who agree with me. Besides, I often quote you when I end up in a discussion again, and I often get people to change their mind about some things.

What I also necessarily need to say is that I really adore your friendship and your love for each other. I have never seen two people together who love each other and their families so unconditionally like you both do. This is such a beautiful example for what love really is.

You are showing everyone that there are no rules or boundaries for love. I really love all of these different facets that love can have and you, again, opened up my eyes. So please, stay forever together. Even when The Fosters will end at some point, please never forget to meet up and tweet some Sherri Polo selfies. This world needs those photos.

So again… thank you, thank you, thank you. Your support means everything to me, and please never forget how many lives you have changed. Being in the closet and not being the person you want to be is pure poison. Sooner or later everyone gets sick from it, and you thankfully saved me from this.

I will always be endlessly grateful for everything you've ever done for all of us and this world in general. I would really love to give something back to you after you did so much for me, and I hope these lines were a good start.

I really love you and hope I can tell you some more things in person someday. The last years have been the most beautiful, honest, heartwarming, funny, and unforgettable years I've ever had. Thanks to you, my Loves. I will never forget you and I promise I will always support you — no matter which way you're going to choose.

Much love from my gay heart and the best regards from Germany,
— Sarah Gante

@SaumSmile

The first time I watched The Fosters was because my cousin was catching up on her shows. So here is little me watching the second episode and Sherri Saum comes onto the screen. I, of course, start freaking out because her hair is EVERYTHING. So, my cousin asked if I wanted to see the first episode.

At first, I thought it was just a TV show but, then I realized how much of an impact it made on me and many others. This show has created friendships, relationships and even families! It is not just a show. It is a family.

— Abigail Prince

Shay Tyann (Twitter account not provided)

To the cast and crew:

You have taught me to accept everyone for who they are. Because of the cast and the show, I have made some lifelong friendships. You have also taught me to believe in myself. You guys are simply amazing. I love each and every one of you. You guys brought a whole new meaning to TV by covering stuff other shows refuse to.

— Shay Tyann

@shebeTae

I found out about The Fosters when I was home one day skipping through channels and trying to find something to watch on TV. I ended up stopping on ABC Family, and the pilot commercial popped up. As I was watching, I saw Sherri, but it didn't click for me that it was her until later. I watched it again and was hit over the head like,

"Wait… KERI REYNOLDS… AND… PAMELA MARTHA FOCKER, TOO?! BOTH OF MY BABIES? TOGETHER?! WHAAAAT?!" I've been hooked ever since.

The thing that attracted me to the show was that it felt like I was seeing my own life and family on the screen. I really appreciated that. It made me feel good to know I'm actually not as alone as I had felt before. I think the thing that connected me so strongly to the show was that I saw my life: past, present, and future. Even more so, I saw my pains. I see myself in every character so much that it scares me. It's done right.

I never thought I'd be given a TV show that would show my struggles and show me how to deal with them and myself properly like The Fosters has. It's also bonding time for my grandma and me. We watch it together and sit and talk predictions for the next episode and season like we're teenagers again.

To me, the best thing about The Fosters is basically everything. I don't know where to start. We have a fandom, and that fandom has done so much from building friendships to raising money for organizations to living out their career dreams. We've even had a long-distance couple GET MARRIED. All through this show.

It would literally leave me heartbroken to see it end, but if I could write the ending, I'd end it with Stef and Lena having grown old together and the kids being full adults with children and out on their own. They'd be sitting together on the porch swing reminiscing about their lives.

The character(s) I connect with the most would be both Stef and Lena. I connect with Stef through her struggles. When I see Frank and Stef, I see my mom and me. I came out to her when I was 18, and I'm just now feeling like I've made my peace with the " backlash " of it all. I'm almost 25 now. I connect with Lena through our love for children. I can meet a child for the first time, and by the end of that day it's like we're best friends. Also, my major in college was Childhood Development.

I connect with Sherri just in life itself overall. Our birthdays are, what I like to call, "an adult and 12 days apart." We're also the same sign (Libra), which I think makes us very similar in character. The actor that influences my life the most is tied between Sherri and Teri. Sherri has influenced me to just keep my good heart and, if there's something eating at my heart, whatever it is, as long as it makes me happy, to follow it. Teri has influenced me in the way that I've realized that I don't have to be ashamed or scared to love or be tolerated by anyone. I deserve to be celebrated for being who I am.

My favorite Sherri tweet is when she said, "I had a nightmare that Tina Turner was chasing one of my sons on a bicycle #Whatisinmywater." I crack up crying laughing every time I read it. I don't start my day without that tweet.

I would like for the entire cast to know that I'm grateful for every last one of them. From working all the long hours away from your families to representing my LGBTQ+ community when we've had no one to do so for so long, it's ALL appreciated. You're all my family, and I LOVE YOU GUYS SO MUCH!

My favorite storylines are: when Stef was shot. I was worried she was gonna die, but she woke up, fought through the pain, and asked Lena to marry her instead. I cried as if she proposed to me lol.

The Lena/Monte storyline AFTER Stef was told everything. It upset me SO MUCH, but I toughed it out bc it gave me #Breese (Bianca and Reese from All My Children) feels. #Breese was my 1st ever lesbian ship, so it basically put me back in my grandma's living room in front of the TV when I was a kid.

Lena losing Frankie. That storyline makes me so sad. Even though I already know what's gonna happen, I still cry whenever I watch Mother. Layla and Frankie the Unicorn tear me up every time.

The Mariana/Nick storyline. I've never experienced anything like that in my own love life, but it was scary. From the time Nick burned the warehouse to Lena panicking about Mariana to Stef running into the school to the end when he was caught, I was on the edge of my seat. I LOVED that episode.

Stef/Tess. I've been waiting for Tess to show up ever since her name was first ever mentioned, honestly. I like that Lena teases Stef about it because it turns her into that 16-year-old again.

My favorite episode is between Under Water and The Long Haul. Under Water is a favorite because it was everything Stef and Lena. The whole episode was just beautiful. The Long Haul is a favorite because Stef and

Lena got married again, and I live for anything Stef and Lena.

My favorite scene is from Consequently when Stef basically humiliated Lena in front of Mike and Lena went crazy with the knife. It wasn't supposed to be funny, but that scene makes me laugh because I've been in Lena's shoes with that.

Question for Sherri: Tupac or Biggie? Why? Favorite song of that person's?

Ending comments: I'd like to say that I used to feel like it was enough for me to just exist, but because of The Fosters, I'm now living my best life. My life is a lot more peaceful, and I'm happier than I've been in a really long time.

— Tyshawn Ransom

@shelcarter17

I'm not even sure where to begin with this. The Fosters has impacted me in so many ways that it would be impossible to put it all on paper or put it into words. However, one of the biggest ways this show impacted my life was by portraying a normal lesbian couple on television. I was amazed that this wasn't some fancy, hip part of LA like The L Word with upper class women. Instead it was just a normal couple with kids, working normal jobs, and leading a normal life. At least the first couple of seasons were normal. Then it seemed to get unrealistic with ALL of the teenage dramatic/political stuff and less and less of the actual normalcy between the mothers and family dynamic. But regardless, the show taught me a lot, and I enjoyed tuning in every week to watch.

Another HUGE way the show impacted me was because of Twitter. I got on Twitter when I first started watching the show after season 1A. I saw that Sherri Saum was on, and I'd tweet her all the time and start interacting with other fans. There is one thing that can't be denied… the fans of this show are FIERCE! We love this show wholeheartedly, and we began to love each other as well. This show leaves behind a myriad of friendships it helped create. I have several close friends that I will go on to have long lasting friendships with even after the show is well over. One of the people who brought all of us together was none other than Teri Polo herself. This woman busted onto the Twitter scene "like a wrecking ball" as we joke at times. But I wouldn't expect anything less from her. She does nothing half-assed.

What started out as silly dares and ways to make people laugh on Twitter turned into lifelong friendships. This wasn't all just because of Teri either. Teri and Sherri are a match made in heaven. The two are a fire and force that captivated many, many hearts. It's because of them that so many of us dedicated fans tuned in every week, and it's because of them that we are sad to see this ending. I know that we all wish them the best and will follow both their careers from here on out.

I'll close with this; For 5 years this show has entered the homes of many, and it opened our hearts to so much. The legacy it leaves behind won't be forgotten. The friendships it has formed in my life I will cherish. I don't feel this is the end. Teri and Sherri's advocacy and love has given us all something to strive for. This is only the beginning.

— Shelby Carter

@SherriTeri_FR

There are some storylines very close to my own life. The first was when Brandon had his hand destroyed and couldn't play the piano like he wanted. Like him, I played and loved piano since I was 8 years old. A few years ago, I fell in the snow and my right thumb was destroyed. Because of this, I couldn't play for one year and now my piano is not as good as before the accident.

The second storyline is when Monte fell in love with her coworker Lena and discovered she was bisexual. Before this story, I always thought I was weird or not normal for loving men and women. I had never seen someone like me before in real life or on a TV show. Seeing this story helped me to being confident and proud to be who I am. It's ok to be bisexual. Like Lena said, "you have the right to be proud, to be yourself. "Thanks to this storyline and thanks to the character Monte, a few months after I had the courage to come out to my family.

For the 3rd storyline, it was very bewildering to see my favorite character living exactly the same health issue as me. In September 2015, it was necessary for me to get a mammogram. For a few months, I refused because I was scared and heard mammograms hurt. My aunt had breast cancer, so I knew what it is. In August 2015 during season 3 episode 10, I saw Stef doing this mammogram and that reassured me. I hesitated and finally got an appointment in November 2015.

Three weeks later, in December 2015, I unfortunately found out that I had the breast cancer gene cancer and would need to do a double mastectomy and breast reconstruction. I am not going into any details, but there were some other complications for this reconstruction. I saw some doctors at the same time season 3B was on air. It was very emotional to see Stef living exactly the same things and having exactly the same doubts and fears. I cried so many times during these episodes. But these episodes helped me so much during these next months.

I got the surgery the June 14, 2016, and now I'm better. I'm totally cancer free since September 2017. I can't thank The Fosters enough for helping during this hard time.

— Marjorie Laforest

@Sid_Onia___

I was looking for a diverse TV series, mainly with bisexual or lesbian storylines. I searched online, and The

Fosters came up with a 5-star rating. I gave it a try and was absorbed by it after the first 20 minutes.

What caught my attention was the fostering system; I never knew much about it, and I had relatives that actually fostered a lot of kids, so that was a good way to learn about it. The show is so beautifully done that I could actually understand the feelings that the characters were facing.

Mostly the lesbian couple storyline made me addicted to the show. I'm still in the process of discovering myself, and this show makes me feel "complete." It is hard to turn these feeling into words.

I think I connect so much to this show because of the love and support it outlines in EVERY SINGLE episode. When I started watching this show, I was facing a difficult time in my life where I decided I had enough of my so-called best friend's betrayal, so I distanced her. This led me to not have many people around to talk and, at times, feeling very lonely and wondering if something was wrong with me instead. It was refreshing to watch how much love was and is concentrated in 45 minutes.

The best thing about this show is the reality of it and how up to date is. It always teaches a little about what is going on in this world at this time. The second-best thing is the strong brotherhood and sisterhood between foster kids, biological kids, and moms; DNA doesn't make a family, love does.

My ending would be seeing Lena become the principal at Anchor Beach and kicking some rich people butts, Stef finally putting detective Grey behind bars, Brandon finally attending Julliard and becoming a well-known pianist, maybe playing in Vienna or some other classic music capital. As per Callie, finally getting her life together and getting into college…although it looks like she wants to get into art school, to me she is a promising lawyer or foster advocate, maybe having her own "Girls United." I picture Jude being an engineer. Mariana could have anything — her character is depicted as a strong woman whom can be whatever she wants, just needing to learn how to keep secrets, at least the family ones.

One of the best outcomes would be Jesus recovering completely from his head trauma and managing his TBI and going off to college with Emma. Last but not least, I'd like to imagine Lena finally carrying her baby, but before this both her and Stef finally going on a well-deserved vacation for at least a week.

The character I connect the most to is Stef and Teri Polo; as she once said, she has a lot in common with her character. I related to Stef because she is a strong woman who is not afraid to speak her mind. She would do anything for her loved ones, even if it means getting into some bigger trouble. She never lets herself be weak, even when she needs to be… everyone needs those kind of moments and keeping it inside only makes it worse.

Teri Polo is also a strong woman, not afraid to speak her mind and act the way she feels most comfortable. Her HRC ally for equality speech was mind-blowing: equality, compassion, and much more. This world needs more people that think the way we do. I can't believe that in 2018 we still have to fight for our freedom.

I guess all of the characters influenced my life in some way. The most important message that I always cherish from this show is that, "it's not where you come from, it's where you belong." I have never felt at HOME when I was at my house, so I travelled a lot. I found myself feeling home anywhere but my own. At a certain point, I wish I was like those people whom are happy staying in one place, but this show confirmed that it is actually something that makes you unique, in all the good and bad ways.

I joined Twitter not longer than a year ago, mostly to be updated on the show. Then I discovered a beautiful fandom which is the Fosters Family. Teri Polo's "stolen picture" with Sherri has to be my favorite tweet, where she wrote, "I love her so." To me, that is one of the most beautiful declarations of love, in any kind of relationship.

It's hard to choose only one storyline to be my favorite. This show highlights so many diverse subjects, which is what makes it so unique and why so many of us relate to it. I have multiple favorite episodes: in season one when Lena's ex is in town, I love how confident Stef is, showing that nothing can get between her and her partner. The first wedding episode, from the beginning to end. In the second season, I loved when Stef and Lena went for their baby moon. During the third season, I loved when they hosted Lena's parents' anniversary; it showed how much Stef and Lena love each other despite the problems between them…that's True Love. Also, I loved the entire episode where Stef and Lena told the kids about the mastectomy.

I loved when Stef's mom said, "I know how you get when you're scared and overwhelmed, you just want to batten down the hatches and to weather the storm alone." I relate to this quote a lot because I am the same way. I'm always there for whoever is in need of advice or anything, but when it comes to my own stuff, I don't let anyone in.

In the same episode, I loved the speech Lena gave Stef when she got back home, "what I love about you is so much more than your body. It is your heart and soul, your mind, your laugh, your courage, your compassion" It made me cry. Also, the swimming pool scene. The second wedding was beautiful too. There are too many episodes that I love...I would end up writing ten pages just listing them all.

Not a question, but a request to whoever is in charge of the content of a series DVD: we need outtakes! I'm pretty sure this would make our fandom very happy...seeing Teri and Sherri and the rest of the cast and crew goofing around would be the best part of each day. (Yes, I watch reruns every day, just to make it a little more perfect.)

I would like all the cast and crew to know how much the fandom loves and admires them. The entire fandom is awesome, but I would have to say Teri and Sherri France is the fan I relate to the most. She was the first one I had a contact with, then I discovered the sweet family that is our fandom.

— Sidonia Demonte

Sifra Verheijden (No Twitter account available)

The Fosters is such an important show to me. I am 23 years old, and this show and the characters in it portray the family that I one day hope to have. I live in the Netherlands, and even though people are pretty open-minded here, it can still be scary to be out and proud.

I found out about The Fosters through a friend of mine during a time when I was still figuring out my sexuality. I can't stress enough how important it was at that moment to have a show that represented me. I finally saw myself and a version of me I hope to become in the future (as a mom and a wife) on screen.

I love watching Stef and Lena act as a couple and seeing all the love and difficulties that come with being married and being mothers. Even though I watch the show for the moms (and for the amazing chemistry between Teri Polo and Sherri Saum), the dynamic of the family is amazing to watch, too, and I like that the show addresses so many difficult topics. It also doesn't hurt at all to be able to look at the gorgeous Teri Polo every week!

Just like Stef, I also had my own internalized homophobia. I was afraid of being out and open about my sexuality. Afraid of the world, afraid of other people's opinions. The show taught me that I am just the way I'm supposed to be. It taught me that I should love me for me and that there is nothing weird or wrong about me.

I wish the show could go on forever, mainly because I just want to see Sherri Saum and Teri Polo on my screen every week, but also because I hope it can show people that they are perfect in the way they are and that they are important and loved. I hope it can help people accept themselves and others and have hope for a better future where they're not judged because of who they are or because of who they love.

— Sifra Verheijden

@steckleberry

I was a late-adopter, so to speak, of The Fosters. The first glimpse I saw was a clip of Teri Polo's "who I love shouldn't be an issue for you or anyone else" scene, which I stumbled upon online somewhere. I couldn't find the show and assumed it wasn't shown in Canada. I eventually found it on ABC Spark early in season 3 and binged the first two seasons on Netflix. That binge established my addiction immediately.

I watch The Fosters for the moms, although I have very little in common with them: no kids, no partner, no wife. If I were younger, I would call Stef and Lena's relationship aspirational, but as it stands, I guess I'd just call it vicarious. I have no love in my life, but I can get it in my eyeballs; I watch a Stef and Lena scene and I feel good. If I have a tough day coming up, I'll watch a scene as I get ready for work and start my day happy.

As much as I feel for Stef and Lena, though, I have an even greater admiration for Teri Polo and Sherri Saum. I was aware of Teri mainly from The West Wing, having seen only the first Meet the Parents movie. To me, she was a competent, beautiful, journeyman actor. Likewise, for Sherri, who really hooked me on In Treatment, was a beautiful, talented actor whose name I didn't exactly know how to pronounce. I watched her where I could, but it was piecemeal. As soon as I saw them in The Fosters, however, it was clear they were not competent: they were remarkable.

I had vastly underestimated Teri and was glad to see so much more of Sherri. I joined Twitter specifically to follow Teri and Sherri, and their wit, humour and interactions did not disappoint. There are myriad videos available of appearances, red carpet events, and promotional interviews, and they all highlight these ladies as lovely, smart, funny, thoughtful professionals.

Most importantly though, they are clearly LGBT allies who don't leave it on the set. This was made clear in their well-deserved mutual Human Rights Campaign Ally for Equality honours.

Their acceptance speeches are amongst my favourite and most frequent videos to watch.

LGBT allies always astonish me. It's pure altruism when their only stake is contributing to a kind, fair, loving society. Teri and Sherri are our allies and that adds another layer to my admiration for them as artists. They're part of the sisterhood now, which means that all future projects get a free look. No matter how long Stef and Lena last, I'm a fan of Teri and Sherri for good.

— Jane Steckle

@SusHe12

I remember it well. I heard about The Fosters only because Joanna Johnson was on The Bold and the Beautiful with Crystal Chappell at the time. Through an interview she talked about Joanna's role in The Fosters. This got my attention, and while I wasn't exactly sure what the show was all about, I soon got to learn the background storyline of this beautiful family.

The connection for me was how diverse and culturally rich the stories were and continued to be with every episode. It blew my mind sometimes at how on pulse the writers were in their storytelling. I was hooked. Almost all the time with each episode (and I missed only two in the entire five seasons), I was either laughing out loud, crying like a baby, or angry as hell. Listen, I'm an old fart, and never has a show impacted me and taught me things that I was oblivious to in such a profound way. Friends comes in a close second, but The Fosters tops it all. I was so incredibly sad when I heard the news that the show was being cancelled. The emotions were real. Like, what was the network thinking?! I digress.

Anyway, there were so many episodes that were exceptional, but the ones that affected me the most personally were the ones when Stef had cancer. Coincidentally we had it at the "same time," and the inspiration that I got through the show and the support I got directly or indirectly from Teri herself was one of many positives that helped me through my journey. The part that resonated the most with me was the time Stef cut her hair and made reference to the peacock giving her a symbol of confidence. I love when she said that having short hair and no boobs didn't define her as being less of a woman. I cheered so hard at that interaction and replayed it in my mind for days. See, I was bald and boobless myself and to hear that played out on TV gave me the confidence that I was okay too. :) I mentioned this to Bradley Bredeweg and jokingly said that It felt like the series was written just for me!

I'm going to miss seeing this show, the cast, and the wonderful storytelling. My heartfelt thanks and gratitude to all that made The Fosters family our family. Specific shout and love to my main man Bradley Bredeweg. To the sensitive and funny Peter Paige. To the genius and awesome director, Joanna Johnson, and last but not least, to the two woman that made this show rock: Sherri and Teri! Praise to their talent as actors, their love for each other off and on screen, their collaborative interactions, and their beauty ... #ourlovesourlovesourloves,

Teri Polo (Stef Adams Foster) and her partner in crime Sherri Saum (Lena Adams Foster).

Peace and Love Always
— Susan Heldsinger

@sylvjwatkins

I found The Fosters only one year ago. My cousin introduced me to the show. He is gay and was telling me about this wonderful show about two moms and their children. From the very first episode when Stef came home and kissed and hugged Lena, I knew I was hooked. Now we are on Season 5, and their love is still just as real and strong.

I connected the most with Stef. I am a carbon copy of her in so many ways. I had the best friend thing like Stef and Tess and didn't know what it was back then. My feelings were unknown and also forbidden in my world.

So yes, I was repressed of my feelings. And yes, I lived most of my life a lie and am only just finding myself and the true me. I owe this to Stef and Lena and the show that I love more than anything!

— Sylvia Watkins

@Tamaraldm

I first found the show because of a video of Sherri and Teri on YouTube. I don't know why I found them, but I also didn't know what my life was about to become because of them! After spending a lot of time watching videos of them, I did some research to see where they were from. I discovered that they were acting together on The Fosters. I read what the show was all about. I knew I really had to watch it because I was going to fall in love with it!

The thing that attracted me was the concept. Seeing a family struggling with a lot of things, seeing a new kind of show that was closer to my life than others, seeing a family that I could relate to was and is very important to me! That's also why I connect this much to the show. As a gay teen I find it very important to see people like me. It made me realize that I wasn't alone at all and that it was possible to have a "normal" life no matter who I am. Every character in this show taught me something, like fighting and standing up for what I believe in is important. It also taught me that it was normal to deal with some teenage things and that if you talk it can get better!

That's what I think is the best thing about this show. What makes it beautiful is the fact that you can almost relate to all the characters no matter if you're straight or not, no matter if you are a foster kid or not, etc. Their stories are relatable. It's real, and I think it's amazing!

For example, I connect in so many ways with Stef and Lena because they show what true love is all about. There is nothing but love, kindness, compassion, and support in their relationship. They have a relationship that is hard to find on television. We can see how much they love each other and how much they need one another, and it's so pure and so beautiful. Love should be shown like that. I think because of that it's easier to relate to them. They are the characters that help me the most in my life. I feel like they are real. I feel so much watching them, struggling with their children and themselves. Despite everything, they still try to fix things. They taught me not to give up every time I wanted to, and they just give me so much strength!

And I would love them to know — not only Sherri and Teri, but everyone — that I hope they realize the impact they can have on people's lives. They mean a lot of things to a lot of people. And mean everything to me. Watching them gave me the feeling that I was at home with them in a way. They were something very important in my life, and they will always be!

Every storyline and episode was amazing. I have never been disappointed by something. Everything was important to me and made me go through all kinds of emotions! I really could cry, laugh, and feel angry all in the same minute. I think that this aspect of the show is also what makes it so real and what makes you feel connected with it!

I also have a question for the cast members: what has the show brought into your personal lives?

I just wanted to say a big thank you to every person that was a part of this, to every person that made that show happen. I wouldn't be in the place that I am right now if I didn't have the show by my side. You helped me in so many ways. You can't imagine how you, the cast members, helped me on a daily basis, so thank you from the bottom of my heart to every single one of you! And I also wanted to say to Sherri and Teri. I am so grateful to have found you. Thank you.

Because of you, I finally accept myself. I can finally be myself completely, and that's so magical. It feels so good. I'm free now and much happier because of you. Because of your characters, of course, but also because of you as humans! So, thank you for making my life better, brighter and healthier. I really don't know what I would do if I didn't have you, and I am so grateful for that! I love you so much!

— Tamara

@TammyVanScoy_

When I was asked if I would like to participate in this tribute book to The Fosters cast and crew, I can honestly say I was honored and nervous at the same time. There is so much I could say to each and every one of you, and so much I want to say, but then it would take away from the other people and what they need/want to say to you. So, I will try to make this short. (Please note I am not leaving names out because I am not thankful for all of you, it is just I only have so much space on this page to include you all. This isn't in any specific order.)

Let me start off with something that is to the writers and cast of The Fosters. I am sure you know who you are when I talk about this. A while ago I made a slam poem type thing, and this is a part of it. (It was pretty much my life summed up in a poem.)

Let's go back to when I started watching this show.
A show with two moms and a big family, the kind of life I've always wanted.
Stef's storyline started fitting my life, like a puzzle finding its last piece.
At the time I started watching the show, I was falling in love with a woman.
As women we knew it was "wrong" to be together in this world.
When Stef told Mike she was in love with Lena,
She made sure he knew it was not his fault.
That was what I needed to say to the man I was with.
Let's go back to the night I told him.
The fear flickering in my fractured soul.
Let's go back to when I knew there was no going back

and everyone had to know.

Now let me take you to the feeling of love and freedom.

The support I got after I was out to the world.

I pushed a restart button to my life.

I gained a whole new group of friends, a whole new family, and what I thought was best of all a wife.

The love of my life.

Or at least what I thought would be the love of my life.

You see, sometimes love can be only one-sided or at least feel that way.

Let's go back to the feeling of, "it was my fault because that is what they would say."

Let's go back to the feeling when I felt like my life was better off when it was taken by a knife.

I felt like there was no need to be here without the one person I loved: my wife.

Let's go back to the support I had when I had to reach out like a person drowning in an endless sea of regret.

Let's go back to my heroes that are still there for me today even yet.

Let's take you to today.

I am in love with a new person, I see things so much better now.

If I could thank anyone it would each and every writer on The Fosters.

Anyone who has ever acted on the show.

Anyone who works with the show.

Anyone in my life that has held me up through the hard things… and lastly,

Freeform for being brave enough to portray diversity and emphasize love in a world that needs it.

So, happily ever after?

Gosh, no.

Powerfully pushing forward?

You bet so.

Even when you feel like water is wading in your lungs,

Just know that you aren't done.

This world needs you more than it ever has before.

I have connected most with Teri Polo and Sherri Saum. They have helped me through some very hard times in my life as well as some very good times.

If I had to pick a storyline that seems like I have connected the most to it would be Stef and Jesus's. I have been through almost the same things as Stef, and I have ADHD like Jesus, and by the looks of it, issues with the ladies like he did as well. But, like both of them, when I love someone I hold on to it as long as I can, and I never give up. Like Lena, I like to teach and stand up for what is right. I am a fighter like Stef and a protector like Lena when it comes to the kids, even when they are not mine.

— Tammy Van Scoy

@TashaBush90

Stef's signature kiss to Lena's forehead always made my heart skip a beat because you just knew Stef was telling her, "forever I'll love you" with a simple kiss to her forehead. It saddens me that the show will not return. TV will never be the same without them...

— Tasha Bush

@TeamBrallie_

Dear David,

I just wanted to thank you for inspiring me. You've helped me understand that things will eventually be okay even if they are not right now. You give me hope that I will be okay.

I am so proud of you. Watching you over the past five years on The Fosters has been absolutely phenomenal.

You make me laugh and cry all at the same time. Brandon shows us that we are all human and it is okay to make mistakes. Hopefully you will be slaying as Brandon for years to come. I cannot wait to see all of the things you accomplish in your career. You are destined for greatness. I do know that no one could portray Brandon Foster better than you.

Thank you for being YOU! I love you so much, GLambert!

All my love,
— Cassie Johnson

@terimyweakness

Hi! Last year my brother and I were looking for a new TV show to watch together because we were bored, and he found The Fosters. I fell in love with the TV show from the first episode. The actors, the history, everything about the show attracted me.

I connected in a strong way to this show because it's the most socially aware current TV show. It talks about real issues: LGBTQA+ issues, immigrants, foster youth and the system, people of color...EVERYTHING THAT MATTERS.

I love the actors. Teri and Sherri are my favourites. The best thing about the show is that it is so positive and based on love and respect. The family aspect is the best thing about the show. I'm rewatching the show because I like it a lot.

If I could write the ending, it would be happy. All the family (the kids, Stef and Lena, Stef's mother, Lena's mother and Lena's father) would be together in a family meeting laughing, eating, and having fun.

My favourite tweet is, "Who I love shouldn't be an issue for you or anyone else… " by Teri. I love that phrase. I would love to meet Teri and Sherri. They're so cute. I'd love to talk to them and take a selfie. I have a question for Teri and Sherri… when are you coming to Argentina?! I need to know you.

My favourite episode is when Stef and Lena reconciled at the party of Lena's parents. My favourite scene is Stef and Lena's kiss in the rain. When Stef cut her hair is one of my favourite scenes, too. She looks amazing.

The Fosters has genuinely given me new eyes for so many things. Sherri and Teri's interviews never fail to make me laugh or smile. They're so funny. I love Teri and Sherri so much.

— Kiara Gilardenghi

@The_Real_Nae101

Hey! My name is Janae Jenkins, but everyone calls me Nae. I started watching The Fosters the moment it came out. I remember watching TV and seeing the commercial. My first thought was, "OMG, they're lesbians just like me." LOL.

I never thought that it would change my life the way it did. Soon it wasn't just about Lena and Stef being a lesbian couple anymore — it was about all the characters and how I related to all of them. For instance, I related to Callie and Jude because they moved so much in their young lives. Having trust issues from all the moving and not feeling like you can trust the people around you or just not wanting to get close to people around you because you felt like it wasn't going to last were feelings I understand. In a way, I also related to Mariana and Jesus when they tried to get close to their birth parents who left their lives due to drug problems. Luckily, I've had my mother in my life, but you also want to fill that void when you have an absent parent.

A show like The Fosters where you can relate to every single character is something very special and something that will be dearly missed. If the show could go on for the next 30 years, I wouldn't miss one episode. Right now, it's like an emotional rollercoaster because there's so much more that I know the show could offer, so for it to end so suddenly makes this a hard change. Lastly, I just want the cast and crew to know that they've helped me so much through dark times, especially through my mental health problems. I just want to say I appreciate you and you've helped me through a lot. I love you all.

— Janae Jenkins

@thedebolson

I first heard about The Fosters sometime in late 2013. I had read that one of the executive producers was Jennifer Lopez (yes!), the main characters were a female couple raising a family (yes!) and that it was on ABC Family (huh?). About the same time, I was dealing with the end of my 17-year relationship and trying to sell our family home while my soon-to-be ex had moved 750 miles away. This new show intrigued me, but I just didn't have the time or energy to watch it. Fast forward to early 2014 – my relationship had ended; the house had been sold and I was lost.

One night something reminded me of The Fosters, so I started watching it. Like so many, I binge watched and then watched the episodes again and again. Suddenly, I was found.

My chest swelled with pride during the pilot when uniformed Stef walks into the kitchen, kisses Lena, and seems hardly bothered when faced with comments from the-just-released-from-juvie Callie. In that moment, I wanted Stef to be my mom. I wanted to be Stef. I wanted to be Lena, so my partner was Stef. Stef quickly became my favorite, my rock, of all the characters. (Having had the pleasure of meeting and spending time with Teri as a result of the show is an added bonus, but that's a story for another time.)

I shed a lot of tears the year before, and here I was crying again… this time they were 'good' tears, with the most significant coming during the episode Saturday, when Stef speaks up to her dad about how much she loves

Lena and their family. To see a woman speaking so passionately about her relationship with another woman on television was nothing short of miraculous, and to some degree, life-saving. It's hard to describe just how life affirming the wedding episode, I Do, was and still is.

As my Twitter bio states, a television show like this would have done me a world of good when I was growing up. To see a gay woman and her relationship positively represented is so incredibly powerful. I can't imagine just how helpful and hopeful it is to the younger generation — it sure helped this ol' broad.

The show isn't perfect. I'm not a fan of the musical episode and certainly hope that Brallie never returns. Sometimes there are too many storylines when all I want is to see Stef and Lena enjoying each other's company and spending time with their family, but I realize that isn't the way things go with a family drama. I love the show, warts and all, and so appreciate that it's on the air, period!

I'm forever thankful to Bradley, Peter and Joanna for The Fosters, and leading the writers, cast and crew on this incredible journey that I hope continues for many seasons.

I'm forever thankful to Teri and Sherri for embracing Stef and Lena with such character and grace. We're all the better for it.

Oh, and thanks to Freeform (aka ABC Family) for putting The Fosters on the air in the first place.

Sorry I doubted you.

— Deb Olson

@TheFosters4322

I was looking for a show to binge watch on Netflix when I came across The Fosters. I had seen the cast names and I had seen Maia Mitchell, who I've loved because of my childhood and Teen Beach Movie. So, I decided to watch it.

I loved it from the first episode. I just felt the love and emotions almost like I was a part of the show. It brought me and some other Fosters fans together, and I made some new friends. The Fosters means a lot to me. The show represents love and equality, which means so much to me and a lot of other people out there. The best thing about the show is the Fosters family. It's just so much drama. I love drama. Also, their strong love for each other, and the moms' love.

I think I connected the most with Mariana (Cierra) because she is kind of a troublemaker. She goes behind her parents' backs, which I do a lot. She cares about her siblings and she likes to have fun, of course. So do I. Mariana always stands up for what she believes in, and I try to, too. I want her to know that she is my favorite person ever. I look up to her. She's my role model. She is a smart and a strong woman. And I love her very much. She influenced me just by being on the show and the things that she has done. My favorite tweet by her was, "Really love reading all these Mariana tweets! It makes me so happy and super grateful to be able to play her. Love you guys."

My favorite storyline is Mariana always standing up for others and for what she believes in. My favorite episode is when they adopt Callie because Jesus comes back and they're all legally related. It's just a happiness overload.

— Isabella

@THINGSSTRANGERS

I started watching The Fosters during its first season, and I instantly fell in love with the inclusiveness of the storylines along with all of the characters and cast! I loved it in secret for about a year, and I finally decided to make a fan account for the show in 2015, which completely changed my life for the better.

My account has changed since then (as have I), but my love and appreciation for the show and what it has brought me still remains! I have a beautiful group of online friends, which I always wanted, who remind me that there are lovely people all around the world.

Without Twitter and the show, I feel that I would be a very different person today. Thank you for such a beautiful show that tells real, current stories with an amazing group of characters to match!

Sincerely,
— Tori

@thisischinahere

To every single person who has made The Fosters the show that it is:

Wow! I can't believe it's been five years since this amazing, groundbreaking show premiered. I can still remember where I was the first time I heard about this show. I was in the mall and saw the promo and was like, "I've gotta watch this show." I began telling my friends and my family as well—basically anyone who would listen.

This show changed the way I thought, related to, and approached LGBTQ people as a straight person. Because growing up I was taught that gay people go to hell. With this show I realized that I was very misinformed. The Fosters began the summer of my 8th grade year back when I wasn't comfortable in my skin or sure about who I was. I'll never forget begging my mom to let me and my siblings stay up until 10 so I could watch the episode.

The show carried me throughout high school as well, and in 2015 I joined the fandom on Twitter. Live tweeting with you all has been a joy! I loved discussing with others in the fandom about the different possibilities that the next episode would bring. I've also loved following y'all in your respective careers.

Being a Houston girl myself, I love the representation that Miss Thang brings to the screens. It was an absolute honor creating the Faded fan video with Lisette and Maddy. You all have inspired me in more ways than you will ever imagine. This great show has inspired me and many others. I can still remember joining in to #RenewTheFosters on more than one occasion, so of course it sucked when I saw the horrible news.

This show was the first place I felt that I truly belonged and could have a voice. You guys have made me find my voice. Now I'm 19 years old typing out a letter to my absolute favs in the business. I really believe that you all have great careers ahead of you, and I can't wait to follow them every step of the way. I'm hoping one day we will be able to meet in person, so I can tell you this in person. From the bottom of my heart, THANK YOU.

— China Louis

@thx4thesave

Witty, warm, wife, "Who I love shouldn't be an issue for you or anyone else."
Hot, hardworking, has handcuffs
Your mom and mine, yonder neighbor's pool

Intense, independent, "I met a woman I can't live without."
Loves with her whole heart, loyal, learning
Optimistic, outspoken, organized
Vulnerable, versatile, valiant
Exciting, encouraging, extinguished Pearson
Strong, sensitive, serious
Tenacious, trustworthy, that short hair!
Empathetic, emotionally intelligent, embraced Callie and Jude
Fierce, forgiving, fixes plumbing
Attractive, amorous, always there for her children
Determined, devoted detective
Affectionate, adventurous, astute
Mom of 5, married 3 times, makes mistakes
Sexy, sarcastic, survivor
First and foremost a mom, five hearts, fearless
Overwhelmed but she persists, on top, on bottom
Smart, sincere, she is Lena's home
Tough love, takes on cancer, twerks
Energetic, economical, eats dinner with Tess and Lena
Real, responsible, removes doors

— Sue Gartenberg

@TiffSmallwood

To me this show was the beginning. The beginning of friendships that I can't imagine not having, the beginning of my obsession with live tweeting, and the beginning of the LGBT community being accepted as parents and people in our world.

The Fosters highlighted things that I have and have not gone through in my life and things that a lot of people ignored. This show wasn't about just one demographic — it was about them all and beautifully portrayed those things weekly. To say I'll miss this show and the amazing cast and crew is an understatement. The Fosters is now and will forever be a part of my heart.

— Tiffany Smallwood

@ToivanenPia

I found The Fosters about year ago on Netflix, more specifically in July 2016. It was LOVE at first sight. After that, The Fosters has been part of every day in my life. My best friend can prove it. ;)

For example, I watch episodes, scenes, or interviews and follow them on Twitter and Instagram. I'm very hooked.

:) I really love this show...it's so incredibly good. The Fosters has taught me about love, and I feel that I've finally found peace in my life.

I love all The Fosters cast and crew. I love the quote, "Who I love shouldn't be an issue for you or for anyone else" by Stef. Most of all I love Stef and Lena... and Teri and Sherri. Teri Polo and Sherri Saum are awesome actors. Their friendship and chemistry are incredibly beautiful. I really respect and adore them very much. There aren't words to explain how much I care about them. "Without Sherri there is no Teri," Teri once said.

It's very difficult to choose which episode is my favourite because every episode is so brilliant. Every episode makes me laugh, cry, think, and hope. So many feelings. "It's not where you come from. It's where you belong."

I'm so grateful for what The Fosters" has brought to my life. It feels like I'm part of the family. I want to thank you all from the bottom of my heart. THANK YOU! Hugs and kisses to all of you from Finland.

I LOVE YOU ALL! "DNA doesn't make a family — LOVE does."

— Pia Toivanen

@toolsforbalance

The Fosters has changed my life, plain and simple. The fact that a positive portrayal of a healthy and very human lesbian relationship was finally in the media changed everything for me and SO many other women!

Up to that point, we were portrayed, much as gay men were — as either total psychos or space aliens and NOTHING in between. Nothing.

Until Bradley and Peter and Joanna put it all on the line to create something so sweet and spectacular, we were all literally starving!

What Sherri Saum and Teri Polo have brought to the table is nothing short of miraculous! I haven't even touched upon the authentic and kind portrayal of foster and adopted children, now that I am one of those co-parents myself!

When most of your life you've had to hide who you are or apologetically explain rather than celebrate and rejoice, having a media oasis that is kind and loving is everything! Love is Love! This show has brought together a worldwide community of gay and straight and lesbian and transgender and foster and adopted people in a conscious and constructive and compassionate way. This has never existed before!

There is literally nothing I could say to any of the producers, staff, or amazing cast that could EVER express my love and gratitude for each and every one of them! Yes, I've obsessed on the mamas like any sane lesbian would, but make no mistake, the rest of the cast is a God send in ways that cannot be properly articulated.

God/dess bless you all!!

All my love forever,

— Heather M. McCrae, MEd

@TPoloPolo

I first heard of the show through a TV ad. My son and I waited patiently for the show to air. We could relate to every episode.

I adopted Shannon through Toronto CAS (Children's Aid Society) when she was 5 1/2 after several foster homes. We watched it together every week and recalled how she/we lived through every issue the Fosters were experiencing. We had done it all. I HAD done it ALL. Only I did it with one child. The Fosters had five! Shannon was a handful for sure. I am a single mom. The longer the child has been in care, the more trauma they have experienced. We had a lot of behaviour modification to do.

The theme song for the show made me cry every week. After five years, I still cry. We did numerous stints of counseling. Whatever this child needed, I found the help. I let Shannon be Shannon, and if that meant wearing boy clothes and playing with boy toys, then so be it.

At 12 years, Shannon came out to me as being a lesbian. Ha, I already knew. Moms know. I should add that we always talked about anything and everything. Nothing was off limits.

At 18, Shannon told me she was transgender. Okay. What do we need to do? Where do we go from here? Firstly, she picked her new name. He now goes by Sam. So, I have had a son for the past two years. We are working on a legal name change, and we just booked a date for his top surgery. Sam has been on testosterone for about a year and a half. He has gained weight, bulked up, stronger than ever. He is a good-looking man of 20. He is my protector. He loves to watch out for me. He has to take this hormone for the rest of his life.

I recently sold our condo and said I would give him his inheritance now before I spend it all. So, I gave him $10,000 for his top surgery. He can't wait to be able to go swimming topless. I am so lucky I can help his dream come true.

We still watch The Fosters, but usually on our own now. And we still compare notes about the show. I think this show is an eye opener for so many people. Showing us the possibilities that await us and the courage we process inside that we didn't know was there.

I think The Fosters played a big role in my own life, too. I came out at age 59. That piece of my life is no longer empty. I never knew the possibility was even there when I was younger. It was not talked about. It was not taught. It was not on TV to see. It was an unknown. I can't even tell you how happy I am now. It's where I belong!

One of my favourite scenes is from the pilot. It is seven seconds and so very powerful. I am talking about Callie's bathtub scene. How many thousands of kids have prayed for this comfort, for this security. A chance to be vulnerable but also a part of something so big. We see a tub with a rubber ducky. They see and feel a safety net, a comfort. They get to experience what so many take for granted.

I think I can relate to Stef's character. I am the disciplinarian. I have to be tough.

— Kathy Walduck

@Uri_naidoo99

Thank you to The Fosters cast and crew, who have helped me get through some of my lowest points. I'm so grateful for this show.

Love,
— Uri Naidoo

@VanesacSanchez_

Hello! My name is Vanessa Sanchez. I first found The Fosters on Netflix. I got attracted to this show because it's the life I want someday, to be in love with someone just as much as Lena and Stef and adopt kids.

I am connected to this show so much because of all the truth that comes out of it. This show brings real life situations to TV screens all across the world. It shines a light on things no one wants to talk about or accept these days.

The best thing about this show is every character has their own struggles, and it's something fans can relate to. Not just gay people — everyone can relate to someone in this show. I personally can relate to Stef's character, how in the beginning her dad didn't want her to be gay and she felt it was only right to marry Mike. My mom doesn't want me gay. She found out about my last two exes and flipped, so I've just been living my life hidden just so I won't disappoint her.

But I also really can relate to Lena's character, how she's so sweet, supportive, loving, caring, and always concerned about others. That's exactly me.

My favorite tweets are always by Sherri. She's my absolute favorite! I always tweet her when it's live tweeting time during the episodes, but I never get noticed lol. But my absolute favorite tweet was by her and it said, "there's no one who can stop you. If you can't go through — go around — go above — dig a path." This tweet has been the motto of my life. I want to say thank you to all the writers for bringing real life problems to the screen and addressing them so well that everyone can relate to them.

Thank you for making a show that keeps fans interested and able to relate to a character or two in every episode. I love this show so much. I can't pick a favorite scene or episode because every scene, every episode is just so good!

-Vanessa Sanchez

@vanitylmj

Dear cast and crew of The Fosters,

I am absolutely sad to hear that The Fosters is coming to an end. I remember being on summer vacation and laying on my bed, wondering what to do. I had just finished binge watching an MTV show, and then I remembered I had told myself to binge watch The Fosters.

The name of the show itself is what attracted me the most. I had originally thought the show was called The Fosters because it would be about kids in the foster system, but then I searched it up and saw the characters' last names were Foster. I ended up watching the show anyway and turns out the show was about kids in the foster system. All the other shows I've ever watched were so fictitious and full of fantasy. For example, how possible can it be to wander through the woods at night with your best friend and end up becoming a true alpha, or that a girl can hold a grudge for so long they come back to torment you and your friends?

When I started watching this show, I never thought that I would ever get so attached to it and to its characters. I can truly say this is the only show that has and will always hold a special place in my heart. I found pieces of myself in Maia's and Cierra's characters, Callie and Mariana Adams Foster. Callie, a young girl who was taken into the foster system alongside her younger brother Jude, found herself forced to grow faster than other kids would. She had to take care of her younger brother, give him the love their foster parents wouldn't, ensure his safety, and act as both a maternal and paternal figure. I found myself in the same situation, except I was seven and doing all those things for my baby brother and two-year-old sister.

I remember sobbing when Callie and Jude's situation was introduced to the audience. That was the moment I knew this show was going to be more important than any other. When I watched the fear in her eyes when she went to rescue her brother from that awful man, I felt it. I felt the fear she felt and for a moment I was Callie, risking it all to save her young brother from living with an awful and violent man. I felt how unfairly she was being treated. Every moment of pain and fear she experienced I felt.

Mariana, a brave, caring and charismatic character who was so determined to do good that situations sometimes ended up bad. I could feel her determination and how upset she got every time her plans went wrong. I too try hard to make things better, but things sometimes just don't go as planned. She was an excellent representation of what it's like to feel different because you look different, so you succumb and change your image in order to feel accepted. Mariana truly was a force to be reckoned with, and I aspire to be as bold and confident as she turned out to be when she tried saving Anchor Beach from going private and when she talked Nick out of doing something that could tarnish his future more.

This show represented the kids in the foster system, the Latino community, the LGBTQA+ community, kids with horrid pasts, kids in blended families; this show was a voice to those who think they are voiceless. The Fosters kept up with current social issues and found a way to talk about it on the show, my favorite being the immigration topic. The amount of energy and empowerment transmitted with each character protesting to keep DACA sent chills down my spine and sent me on an overdrive of emotions. Each episode held a beautiful message of family, friends, love, support and unity. I learned that united we cannot be divided, that our voices do matter, and that it's okay to feel different, to be different. For this and so much more, I will be eternally grateful for the cast and crew of The Fosters.

Sincerely,
— Erika Munguia

@whoswen

First of all, I want to thank the cast/crew for the amazing show. It helps so many people, and it's so important for us. Seriously, I don't know if you guys have any idea how much this show means to some people and how it changed our lives. It's incredible, and I hope you know that.

When I watched the pilot for the very first time, I fell in love with Stef and Lena. I knew I would. I always saw people talking on Twitter about The Fosters, and I was very curious about it. That's how I found my favorite TV show. On Twitter. Seeing everyone talking about how magic it was.

I couldn't believe until I watched it. I'm bisexual, and when I saw Stef talking to Mike about how she feels about women, I saw myself in there. I'm very much like Stef. I'm always showing everyone that I'm strong and that I can handle everything, but sometimes I'm scared and don't want anyone to worry because I think I can fix everything. Stef is so protective just like me, and she's always trying to make people feel better about themselves.

I'm thinking about the ending, and I don't want it to be over. This TV show is so important! I would love to see

Stef and Lena getting old with grandchildren, living in the same house, watching movies, and taking care of each other. But I don't really want to think about it as an end. I think it's just the beginning of a new age, where people are more receptive and respectful.

I love to think about The Fosters because I remember that I met one of my closest friends, Leticia (@danversgirls). I met her because of Sherri. She followed us the same day, and we think it was because of our bio that said, "protect Sherri Saum and Teri Polo at all costs."

I'm very grateful, because if it wasn't for The Fosters (and especially Sherri Saum) I don't know if I would have met this amazing girl. I'm so glad I can call her my friend. (We also have a Twitter account called @portalfosters. We're from Brazil and we translate and post every update of The Fosters to all of those who don't know English. We're always trying our best.

Before I finish, I want to say I love the wedding episode (both). It's so amazing how Sherri and Teri show us how Stef and Lena love each other and how they really want to be together. I also love when they talk about something so delicate so subtly. For example, that scene where Lena is talking about homophobia with Jude in the first season. I love this scene so much, and I think it's one of the best.

As I said, I'm from Brazil (Rio de Janeiro), and I already met Maia here, but I'd love if you guys could come to visit. It's an amazing country, and I know you are all going to love it.

I'm going to thank you all again and again. Thank you so much for this amazing, incredible, and important show. We're all in this together, fighting for a better world and against all kinds of hate.

I want to thank Sherri Saum for being an amazing woman and for always being so kind with me. I hope you remember me.

I want to thank all the cast/crew for making this show for us and for always being available to answer our questions. Teri and Sherri, I love you girls so much. You deserve the world, and I hope someday we can meet.

Maia, Cierra, Noah, Hayden, and David, you guys are AMAZING. We can feel the passion that you have acting, and I love you with all my heart. Peter Paige and

Bradley Bredeweg, thank you, just thank you. If I could give an award for creating the best TV show ever, you guys would be the winners. All the cast and crew, thank you for making this happen!

My name is Julia, also known as @whoswen.

— Julia Petillo

@workinggirl92

I think what makes The Fosters so special is that it brought so many people from all different backgrounds and parts of the world together. It has such a dedicated fan base because it is clear to us fans that the writers and actors really care and put their hearts into every word. They created a family that will last forever!

— S

@xpizzaislifex

Teri and Sherri,

Thank you so much for being you. You guys helped me get through some of the hardest times in my life including when I came out to my mom. You wonderful women gave me the strength to be myself and stay true to myself. I've been a fan since day one, and I'll continue to support both of you as you continue your journeys. I love you both so much! Thank you for a wonderful 5 years of The Fosters.

Love,

— Jonna

@Yaiesha1

I am an absolute huge fan. I love the show so much. This show gives a lot of meaning to the topics that you guys talk about. I love how you are all spreading awareness and showing it's okay to be who you are and not have to hide it from anybody. Simply just be yourself!

I just finished season 5 of The Fosters, and I literally cried during some episodes. This show shows so much emotion and love. That's what I love most about this show. no matter the situation, no matter the consequences, and no matter how hard things get, you all work together and are there for one another as a family should be! I love you guys!

— Yaiesha Gonzalez

@yeppers99

The Fosters is a show that I consider to be home. It is a show that I have no problem praising and encouraging others to watch. I can remember the first time that I saw a promo for the show. I was so intrigued. I first started the show the summer before heading into high school, and it still plays a major role in life while I am in college.

I was first drawn to the show because I was told by my parents that I shouldn't watch it, but that only made me more curious. Just know that finding this show changed my life for the better. It showed me that I wasn't alone and that others felt the same way that I did, and I was able to bond with them.

You guys honestly allowed me to meet my best friends that I FaceTime and text every single day. You allowed me to interact with others who cared about me from thousands of miles away like Rae Ann, who I'm so grateful for. I love that she's giving me a chance to tell you all how I feel about you. I am also so grateful to you all because you all shared episodes that I could find some relation to.

Starting with Cierra's character, I see a lot of myself in Mariana. I still struggle today with finding myself and trying to fit in, but you guys helped me see that others feel this way too and it isn't just me. I remember seeing Mariana struggle with her identity because of her ethnicity, and I felt that so hard because I live in an area where my peers don't really look like me. It was kind of hard to bond because the first thing that some see is color and they aren't so open to forming relationships with people who are different than them on the outside. I like that I could see myself when Mariana felt the same way.

I also found myself in Stef and Lena when it came to the relationship with my parents and trying to please them and live up to their expectations. This show allowed me to discover my favorite actress in the entire world. I know that some try to stay away from the title "role model," but Sherri Saum is one who I look up to immensely. She's a humanitarian whose light shines so bright. Whether it's supporting Kusewera or helping Puerto Rico, she always doing something to help. I love how involved she is and how interactive she is with fans. TBT to when she would join in on our Twitter debates, one being the notorious pear vs potato debate.

Whenever I am feeling just a tad bit down, I go back to her sassy and pun-filled tweets, and just looking at them brings me some joy.

My favorite Twitter memory is when I wrote her a letter, and SHE RESPONDED. I literally had a mini heart attack in Algebra 2, because I was shook that she received it and responded, "Thanks sweet girl!" (Cheesy, I know, but one of my favorite moments because she took the time to read and respond.)

Oh, and don't even get me started with Teri freaking Polo! I can remember the whole fandom joining together to try to get Teri to join Twitter, and when we succeeded, there was a feeling of unity. The time that she spent on Twitter was one that I enjoyed because she shared so much wisdom and positivity. She cares so much, and I appreciate her huge heart. Sherri Polo were and still are my friendship OTP, and I love being able to fangirl every time that they are together at an event. Every Sherri Polo sighting had the fandom fangirling. Watching them both receive awards for being "Allies of Equality" brought me to tears because I too believed that they deserved recognition for all that did, and I was and am still so proud to call them amazing role models.

Getting back to The Fosters, I connected to this show because it's about family. I felt like I belonged to the community and it helped me grow as a person. Although I considered myself to be pretty up-to-date with current events, The Fosters was another place where I got news. Let me just say that this show is so freaking timely. They come up with storylines, and somehow the world follows them almost to the T.

I am constantly shooketh. I absolutely loved every single episode to the point where I would watch it when it first appeared on Monday then I would watch it once a day until the following week. (Pretty excessive, I know, but I was dedicated.) My top five episodes include: The Pilot, I Do, Padre, Mother, and Lucky. They were all such emotional episodes that made me love the Foster family so much more.

I want to thank Bradley, Peter, Joanna, Megan, Wade, Kris, Dan, and the entire cast and crew for their hard work and their amazing writing skills. You are all so talented and I appreciate all that you have put in to provide us with the best show in the world. I am proud to be a fan and I truly love all of you so much even though I have yet to meet you.

CONGRATULATIONS ON THE FOSTERS REACHING 100 EPISODES!!!!

Love,
— Sandlynn Hepburn

@ZENDAYAFANARMY / @TeripoloUpdates

Dear Teri Polo,

My name is Marlaya Williams. The thing that I was the most attracted to while first watching The Fosters was you and the relationship your character Stef was in. My first time watching the show was maybe my 9th grade year. At the time, I was still very much in the closet. It was also really hard to find good representation for myself (being a black queer woman) on TV, and I was always dumbfounded when I would see the same white hetero people on TV.

Most of the time I'd watch The L Word over and over again just for a little slither of LGBTQA+. I had heard about The Fosters mostly because I stanned someone from Disney (Zendaya) and Maia had been on a few Disney movies. Through that, I knew of her and of this new show she was on.

One day I was finally told about the two moms, and I watched the first episode in my basement on my laptop. It took me maybe 20 secs to fall in love with you and 0.2 seconds to fall in love with the TV moms you and Sherri Saum so greatly portray. Watching the show made me feel special and not alone. Watching the show made me feel like my soulmate was somewhere in the universe and I would find them.

Watching the show made me feel like who I am and who I choose to love is okay! I'll never forget one of your most iconic lines, "I fucking believe in love," and man, so do I. When I started watching the show I was maybe 14. I am 19 now going on 20, and I'm really happy that Stef got to be a part of my journey. I'm really happy that you got to inspire, teach, and show me that love has no boundaries. Sometimes you may find love in weird places, but that doesn't make it any less lovely then before.

I am thankful for the entire cast who has taught me many different things in many different ways. But overall, I am just thankful to have supported you and loved you with all my heart. You made me brave, you made me strong, you made me not want to take my own life anymore. And for that, I'm forever grateful.

Love,
— Marlaya Williams